A Catechism of Astrology

A Catechism
of
Astrology

Dr. B. V. Raman

MOTILAL BANARSIDASS
INTERNATIONAL
DELHI

Delhi, 2026

© Motilal Banarsidass International
All Rights Reserved

ISBN : 978-82-19394-75-3 (HB)
ISBN : 978-82-19394-91-3 (PB)

Also available at :

MOTILAL BANARSIDASS INTERNATIONAL

41 U.A. Bungalow Road, (Back Lane) Jawahar Nagar, Delhi-110007
4261/3 (Basement), Ansari Road, Darya Ganj, New Delhi-110002
Shop#. 6, 241, Luz Ginza Complex, Luz Corner, Mylapore, Chennai - 600004
12/1A, 2nd Floor, Bankim Chatterjee Street, Kolkata - 700073

Stockist : Motilal Books, Ashok Rajpath, Near Kali Mandir, Patna-800004

Printed in India by
MOTILAL BANARSIDASS INTERNATIONAL

Foreword

It gives me immense pleasure to note that a fresh edition of my father Dr.B.V.Raman's two-part book *A Catechism of Astrology* is coming out soon. This is one of the best books for learners, especially for beginners, that explains in great detail several of the astrology and astrology-related astronomy concepts in simple lucid language. Most of the content has appeared in the pages of the now defunct The Astrological Magazine of the 50's and 60's and possibly a little later too . What is attractive about this book is the simple approach to astrological concepts which are presented in question and answer format. What many readers may not be aware of is that most of the content was written by Dr.Raman himself under different pennames such as Mihira, Bhattotpala, Leon etc., in the pages of *The Astrological Magazine* in the sixties and seventies.

I should say Mr.Abhishek Jain of Motilal International is doing yeomen service to the cause of Jyotisha by bringing out this fascinating book making Dr. Raman's answers to commonly asked questions available to posterity.

I thank Mr.J.P. Jain and Mr.Abhishek Jain for coming forward to publish this title after a hiatus of more than three decades.

Bengaluru   **Gayatri Devi Vasudev**
April 23, 2025.

Preface to Fourth Edition

Astrological predictions play an important part in man's life. Astrology can predict with fair accuracy important events in life. An experienced astrologer does not just make generalisations from past observations. He has, designed for him, a set of rules, based on intuition and observations extending over thousands of years. There are processes which when carefully and properly handled can enable one to make correct predictions. Often the complex astrological rules are capable of different interpretations, the correct ones depending upon the astrologer's experience and intuitive capacity.

Answers for questions like "which planet causes surgical operations - Mars in the 8th or Ketu in the 8th?", "What is the basis for the allotment of different portfolios to planets in Mundane Astrology?", etc., cannot be found in any textbooks on Astrology. But such topics have been exhaustively dealt with in this volume - tough questions bearing on vocations, yogas, muhurta, female horoscopy and miscellaneous subjects have been answered deftly and with clarity enabling the readers to get an intimate appreciation of the subtler aspects of Astrology so that one can handle a horoscope with imagination and precision.

This volume is in response to the great demand that a combined edition of both the I and II parts of the Catechism of Astrology be issued.

Both volumes together deal with a large variety of commonly asked questions related to Astrology and are bound to provide a great deal of information to the reader.

The Publishers deserve to be thanked profusely for having brought out this combined volume in a attractive form.

Dr. B. V. Raman

"Sri Rajeswari"
Bangalore-560020
1st February, 1992

CONTENTS

Part-I

Chapter-I : General   3

Chapter-II : Concerning the Bhavas   20

Chapter-III : Marriage   57

Part-II

Chapter-I :Vocation   79

Part-I

Part-I

CHAPTER - I

General

Q. 1. What are Perigee, Apogee, Perihelion and Aphelion of the planets?

Ans. When the distance of the Sun (or the Moon) from the earth is least, it is Perigee. When the distance is greatest, it is Apogee. Similarly, the point of a planet's orbit closest to the Sun is Perihelion and the point farthest from the Sun is Aphelion. These cannot be discerned by the eye, for the observer has to locate a planet or a heavenly body only by its Right Ascension and Declination. All the other co-ordinates have only to be derived by spherical trigonometrical transformations.

At certain favourable positions as transits, occultations, etc., which occur when the planet is at a Perihelion or Aphelion position in its own orbit, the ratio of the distances of the planet and the Earth from the Sun or the Moon may be arrived at with advantage.

Q. 2. Why does a solar eclipse not appear at every New Moon or a lunar eclipse at every Full Moon?

Ans. In a solar eclipse, the Moon intervenes between the Sun and Earth. Hence it is obvious that a solar eclipse can only occur at or near conjunction. If the Moon's orbit actually or very nearly coincided with the ecliptic, solar eclipses would recur at every New Moon, but the inclination of the Moon's orbit (about 5° 9') gives to the Moon a latitude which, at the instant of conjunction, is sufficient to keep the two discs apart, unless they, at the same time, happen to be at or near a node (Rahu or Ketu).

In a lunar eclipse, the conditions are as follows: The Moon's light is derived from the Sun and when the earth intervenes itself between the two, it cuts off the sunlight. This can therefore be only on the occasion of a Full Moon. But the Moon's orbit being inclined to the ecliptic at an angle of 5° 9', the latitude of the Moon may be such as to enable it to pass the shadow without entering it, which explains why there need not be a lunar eclipse at every Full Moon. It can therefore occur on a Full Moon only if she is near or at a node of her orbit.

In order that a solar eclipse may be possible, the-angular distance of the Sun's centre from the node at the instant of conjunction must not exceed 18° 36' and if the distance is less than 13° 42', an eclipse occurs.

A lunar eclipse can take place provided the distance from the node at the moment of the full Moon is less than 9°. An eclipse is impossible if this distance exceeds 12° 30'.

An essential distinction between the solar and the lunar eclipses is this: In the one, the luminary is merely hidden from us; in the other, it actually loses its light. The character of a solar eclipse varies from observer to observer, whereas in a lunar eclipse all parts of the hemisphere facing the Moon will see the eclipse and in precisely the same phase.

Therefore, in order that an eclipse should take place, there should be a Full Moon or a New Moon and the specified ecliptic limit should be satisfied. This cannot obviously be at every Full Moon or New Moon.

Q. 3. A day is divided into 12 Rasis or signs each comprising roughly of 5 ghatis. What is the exact period of each Rasi? Discuss with reference to place and season.

Ans. A day in astronomical or astrological parlance is the interval between sunrise and sunset in a particular place for a particular day. That is never divided into 12 Rasis of 5 ghatis each. If 'day' is meant to include 'day and night', even then it is not correct to say that it is divided into 12 Rasis of 5 ghatis each. The zodiac is divided into 12 signs of exactly 30 degrees each. There is at no time any variation in this. But the time taken by each sign to rise in the horizon always varies with respect to place (latitude) and season (month). Whenever the Sun rises in the East, the sign or Rasi occupied by it also necessarily rises at the same time. That sign is a moment in time, the Sun will be occupying only a particular degree of that sign then and that degree is the rising degree or ascendant. Owing to the axial rotation of the earth, this point is apparently pushed up in the heavens at the rate of roughly one degree for every four minutes of time (360° for 24 hours). So at about two hours after sunrise, the Sun would have travelled up about 30 degrees or one sign. Hence, the average duration of a Rasi on the horizon is 60/12 = 5 ghatis. This duration will be different for different latitudes. It varies with season and the average time taken for a sign to rise, i.e., pass over the horizon is 2 hours. The time taken by Aries to rise at London (51° N. 32') is only about 50 minutes and for Libra, it is nearly 2 hours and 50 minutes for the same place. Within India itself at Cape Comorin, the time periods for Aries and Libra to rise are about 1 hour and 52 minutes and 2 hours 3 minutes respectively. The periods of time at Simla for the above two signs respectively are 1 hour 30 minutes and 2 hours 28 minutes. Because of this difference 'day' is sometimes longer and sometimes shorter in the same place at different times of the year. It is different for different places also. But day and night are always together equal to 60 ghatis.

Q. 4. How do you calculate the sthambhana (stagnation) of Mars?

Ans. The ancient books on Hindu Astronomy have given values of the angles subtended at the Sun by two imaginary lines joining the Earth and the Sun and the planet when the planet will appear to be stationary. These have to be essentially rough for the values employed are the mean values of the Radius

Vectors. In the case of Mars and Mercury due to their high value of the eccentricities of their orbits, the radius vectors fluctuate considerably. Hence the sthambhana or stationary point can be arrived at only by comparing the true geocentric velocities (got as the difference between consecutive sphutas) and by fixing that moment when the velocity becomes zero.

Q. 5. How do you calculate the distance of a place, East or West of Ujjain in Yojanas, given the geographical longitudes?

Ans. The difference of longitudes East or West to Ujjain is converted into Yojanas at the rate of 1 degree being equal to 8 8/9 yojanas. For example, Aligarh would be 20 yojanas East.

Q. 6. How do you find the strengths of planets without mathematical calculations?

Ans. There are no easy-chair methods which enable one to measure the strengths of planets without recourse to mathematics. However, the following procedure may be adopted with advantage.

Sthanabala or positional strength is obtained by the planet being placed in exaltation, own house, moolathrikona, friendly house and own Vargas. Jupiter and Mercury obtain Directional Strength (Digbala) in the ascendant (east); the Sun and Mars in the 10th (north); Saturn in the 7th (west); and Venus and the Moon in the 4th (south). The Sun and the Moon get Cheshtabala, in their northerly course (Capricorn to Gemini) and Mars, Mercury, Jupiter, Venus and Saturn in retrogression. The Moon, Mars and Saturn have Kalabala (temporal) strength during night; while the Sun, Jupiter and Venus are powerful during day. Mercury has Kalabala always. Malefics and benefics have Kalabala in the dark and bright halves respectively of the lunar month. Planets in their week-days, months etc., are powerful. Aspects of benefics give good Digbala while malefics give the reverse. The Sun, the Moon, Venus, Jupiter, Mercury,

Mars and Saturn are strong in order (Naisargikabala). The Sun is the most powerful and Saturn, the least.

By applying the above principles one can measure the strengths of planets, of course, approximately.

Q. 7. Nowadays some people, after the fashion of westerners, take into account what are called the heliocentric positions of planets. Are they right in doing so?

Ans. Heliocentric means from the centre of the Sun, while geocentric means from the centre of the earth. Astrology is essentially a science of relativity. It deals with man's relationship with his cosmic environment, the relationship that is properly predicted upon man's existence as a creature of the earth. Since we are concerned with the effects of planets on the earth and not on the Sun, there does not seem to be enough justification for considering the positions of planets from the center of the Sun. Of course, it is a fashion with a few Indians to imitate what all is western - habits, customs, ideas and everything. It is proper and logical to consider the positions of planets relative to the earth.

Q. 8. Explain how to calculate the positions of Upagrahas, Mandi, Dhuma and others.

Ans. Roughly speaking, the position of Mandi will correspond to the degree of the ascendant rising at the following times in the different weekdays, provided the durations of day and night are equal (night=day 30 ghatis).

Week Day	During Day (From Sunrise) At the end of	During Night (From Sunset) At the end of
Sunday	26 Ghatis	10 Ghatis
Monday	22 Ghatis	6 Ghatis
Tuesday	18 Ghatis	2 Ghatis

Wednesday	14 Ghatis	26 Ghatis
Thursday	10 Ghatis	22 Ghatis
Friday	6 Ghatis	18 Ghatis
Saturday	2 Ghatis	14 Ghatis

The figures have to be proportionately increased or decreased accordingly as the duration (of night or day) is greater or less than 30 ghatis. For example, the position of Mandi is required in case of a person born on 8-8-1912 at ghatis 35 after sunrise. The duration of night is Gh. 28-10. Week-day being Thursday, and birth having occurred in the night, the position of Mandi will be at the end of ghatis 22 (from sunset) provided the duration of night is 30 ghatis. Since here the extent of night is Gh. 28-10 (1690 vighatis) the position of Mandi will be as at

$$28\text{-}10 \,/\, 30 \times 22 = \text{Gh. } 20\text{-}39.$$

The ascendant rising at Gh. 20-39 (after sunset) is about Gemini 12° 12' and consequently the position of Mandi is 12° 12' Gemini. The position of Dhuma is found by adding 133° to the Sun's longitude. Patha is ascertained by subtracting Dhuma from 360°. Patha increased by 180° gives Paridhi. 360° diminished by the longitude of Paridhi, gives Indrachapa. Add 17° to Indrachapa and the position of Sikhi is obtained.

Q. 9. How do you find out whether a planet is Asta (setting) or Udaya (rising) and what are the effects on markets?

Ans. Every almanac published in India gives the days when planets become Asta or Udaya. If, however, you want to know the astronomical basis, see Chapter 9 of Suryasiddhanta, the famous work on Hindu Astronomy. Jupiter, Mars and Saturn, when their longitude is greater than that of the Sun, go to their setting in the West; when it is less, to their rising in the East. So likewise, when Venus and Mercury are retrograde. When Venus and Mercury are not retrograde, they go setting in the East when of less longitude than the Sun; when of greater, to their rising in the West.

The degrees of setting are: for Jupiter 11; for Saturn 15; for Mars 17; for Venus the setting in the West and the rising in the east take place at 8 degrees. The setting in the East and the rising in the west take place at 10 degrees. Mercury makes his setting and rising at a distance of 12 or 14 degrees from the Sun, accordingly as he is retrograding or rapidly advancing.

Q. 10. The longitudes (sphutas) of Upagrahas-Dhuma, Vyathipatha, Parivesha, Indradhanus, and Upaketu-are correlated to that of the Sun. What about the movements of Yamakanta and Ardhaprahara?

Ans. The position of Dhuma is found by adding 4 signs 13 degrees and 20 minutes to the figures for the Sun. Subtract Dhuma from 12 signs. The result is Vyatheepatha. This increased by 6 signs becomes Parivesha. When Parivesha again is subtracted from 12 signs we get Indradhanus. So, the longitude of the Sun is the foundation for all these Upagrahas. But Yamakanta and Ardhaprahara are calculated differently and have no connection with the longitudes of the Sun. The basis of their calculation is the week-day. The position of Yamakanta during the daytime on week-days is at the end of ghatis 18, 14, 10, 6, 2, 26 and 22 and of Ardhaprahara at the end of ghatis 14, 10, 6, 2, 26, 22 and 18 beginning from Sunday. Of course, these figures hold good when the days last exactly 30 ghatis and they will have to be proportionately increased or decreased accordingly as the length of the day chosen is greater or less than 30 ghatis

Q. 11. How do you calculate the 12 Avasthas, viz., (1) Sayana, (2) Upavesana, (3) Netrapani, (4) Prakasana, (5) Gamana, (6) Agamana, (7) Sabha, (8) Agama, (9) Bhojana, (10) Nrityalipsa, (11) Kautuka and (12) Nidra.

Ans. Apart from the above 12 Avasthas, there are the other ten Avasthas (vide HINDU PREDICTIVE ASTROLOGY) such as Deeptha, Swastha, Muditha etc. The Avasthas mentioned in the question play an important role in limiting and enlarging the functions of Bhava lord who is subject to the Avastha concerned. Note the number of the constellation (Aswini etc.) in which the planet (whose Avastha is desired) is situated. Note the number of the planet and also note the degree the planet occupies. Find the product of these three. To this, add the number of the person's Janma Nakshatra, the number of the Janma Lagna and the number of birth ghatis from sunrise. Divide the total by 12. The remainder represents the Avastha beginning from Sayana.

Example: (Sun's longitude) Cancer 23°; Sun's Nakshatra Aslesha 2; Janma Lagna Aquarius; Janma Nakshatra Mrigasira; Birth ghatis 35.

(a) The number of the Nakshatra
    (in which Sun is situated)   - 9
(b) Number of the planet (Sun in this case)   - 1
(c) Number of the degree
    (in which the Sun is placed)   - 23
                        Product of the above   - **23**
Add: Number of Janma Nakshatra   - 5
        Number of Janma Lagna   - 11
        Number of Birth Ghatika   - 35
                                                        258

Dividing this by 12, we get a remainder of 6. Therefore, the Sun's Avastha is Agamana.

The results of these Avasthas should be predicted by a consideration of the Drishtis (a special kind of aspect) to which the planet in the Avastha in question is subject to. For more details, reference may be made to Hora Ratna.

Q.12. Kindly illustrate how to calculate the Upagrahas like Bhukampa etc.

Ans. Add 2 Rasis and 20 degrees to the longitude of the Sun at birth, we get Bhukampa Sphuta.

Add to this 1 Rasi and 10 degrees, we get Ulka.

Add 2 Rasis 6 degrees and 40 minutes, we get Brahma Danda.

Add 2 Rasis and 20 degrees and we get Dhwaja.

Add to this 3 Rasis, 3 degrees and 20 minutes and we get the original Sphuta or longitude of the Sun.

Add 2 Rasis 20 degrees to the Sun's longitude (27-30) at birth, we get Bhukampa (3-17-30). Add to the above 1 Rasi 10 degrees and we get Ulka (4-27-30). Add to the above 2 Rasis 6 degrees and 40 minutes and we get Brahma Danda (7-4-10). Add to the above 2 Rasis and 20 degrees and we get Dhwaja (9-24-10).

For verification, if you add to the above 3-3-20, we get the original Sun's Sphuta at the time of birth. Thus, Bhukampa-Kataka; Ulka-Simha; Brahma Danda- Vrischika; and Dhwaja-Makara.

Q.13. How do you find out Beeja and Kshetra Sphutas in the horoscopes of husband and wife?

Ans. There are several methods to find out these Sphutas but I give below only the most common ones. Among these three, the third one is considered to be the most important.

(i) Beeja Sphuta (male horoscope)-Add the longitudes of the Sun, Venus and Jupiter and the sum gives the Beeja Sphuta.

(ii) Multiply the Sun's longitude by 4 and of Venus and Jupiter by 3 and the products when totalled give the Beeja.

(iii) Multiply each of the above three planets by 27 and the sum of the products shows the position of Beeja Sphuta.

Kshetra Sphuta (Female horoscope): Substitute Moon, Mars and Jupiter respectively in the place of the planets mentioned for Beeja and you get Kshetra Sphuta.

Q. 14. How do you calculate Kshanika Grahas in a horoscope?

Ans. Kshanika Grahas are supposed to be 'shadows' of planets-momentary planets-hovering temporarily in the heavens. They are only of symbolical significance and are arrived at by certain mathematical manipulations of birth. The Kshanika Grahas (K. S.) are largely used in horary astrology. First what is called Thihya Sphuta is obtained and from it are ascertained the other Kshanika Grahas. The various principles given in ancient classical works may be reduced to the following general formulae.

Thihya Sphuta (T. S.) in terms of Rasis = Birth time in Ghatis x 36

Diurnal duration.

T. S. Plus 75° = Kshanika Sukra (K. S.)

120° - T. S. = Kshanika Kuja (K. K.)

165° - T. S. = Kshanika Rahu (K. R.)

210° - T. S. = Kshanika Sani (K. R.)

240° - T. S. = Kshanika Chandra (K. C.)

T. S. Plus 300° = Kshanika Budha (K. B)

T. S. Plus 345° = Kshanika Guru (K. G.)

Multiply the ghatikas after sunrise by 36 and divide the same by the duration of day. The quotient is Rasi; the remainder when multiplied by 30 and divided by diurnal duration, gives the degrees. The remainder when multiplied by 60 and divided by the day-duration gives Thihya Sphuta. Add 2 Rasis and 15 degrees to Thihya Sphuta, you get Kshanika Sukra.

Deduct Thihya Sphuta from four Rasis, you get Kshanika Kuja. Deduct Thihya Sphuta from 5 Rasis and 15 degrees and you get Kshanika Rahu. Deduct Thihya Sphuta from 7 Rasis, you get Kshanika Sani. Deduct Thihya Sphuta from 8 Rasis, you get Kshanika Chandra. Add Thihya Sphuta to 10 Rasis, you get Kshanika Budha. Add Thihya Sphuta to 11 Rasis 15 degrees, you get Kshanika Guru Sphuta.

Q. 15. What are superior and inferior planets?

Ans. Mercury and Venus are inferior planets because they are nearer to the Sun than the earth. Mars, Jupiter and Saturn are superior planets, because they are farther from the Sun than the earth. As observed from the earth, the inferior planets come to occupy twice the same longitude as the Sun, that is, while moving on the side of the sun away from earth, and while moving between the Sun and the earth. In the former case, they are said to be in superior conjunction with the Sun and in the latter case in inferior conjunction with the Sun. When the superior planets come to occupy the same longitude as the Sun on the side of the Sun away from the earth, they are said to be in conjunction with the Sun. When diametrically opposite the Sun with the earth in between they are said to be in opposition with the Sun. There is no opposition in case of inferior planets, for their orbits around the Sun being smaller than that of the earth, they are not seen to move sufficiently apart from the Sun as to be on the side of earth away from the Sun. And there is no inferior conjunction in the case of the superior planets, for their orbits around the Sun being larger than that of the earth, they are not seen to move sufficiently close to the Sun as to be between the earth and the Sun. These superior and inferior conjunctions are important when considering chestabala or motional strength of planets.

Q. 16. Is there any relation between Palmistry and Astrology? Which is more accurate?

Ans. This is like asking whether Ayurveda or Allopathy gives better results. Both are accurate in the hands of experts

Palmistry is closely allied to astrology. Astro-palmistry is an important branch of Palmistry.

Q. 17. Can the method of depicting the Nirayana horoscope by Parasari Dasa method be applicable to Sayana ones?

Ans. The rules for interpreting Parasari Dasa results cannot be applied to Sayana system. The Sayana horoscope should be converted into a Nirayana one by subtracting the necessary Ayanamsa.

Q. 18. How can we definitely know from a given horoscope whether it belongs to a living or dead man?

Ans. Generally horoscopes of a living man alone are presented for examination. If, however, one wishing to test the knowledge of the astrologer presents the horoscope of a dead person, the astrologer should be guided by 'Nimithas'. One who has mantrasiddhi will be guided by his Ishta Devata. A careful examination will reveal the longevity and from this also the astrologer can ordinarily judge whether the horoscope is that of a living or dead person.

Q. 19. Have Upagrahas like Mandi any retrograde movements?

Ans. Upagrahas are symbolical points determined according to certain mathematical conventions (See Q. 10). They have no astronomical basis or retrograde motion like Rahu and Ketu.

Q. 20. What are Navadoshas?

Ans. In fact, there are 16 doshas in all. They are Sthuna, Kantaka, Rakta Sthuna, Vishaghatika, Vishti Karana, Gandanta, Vaidrita, Latta, Parivesha, Vyatheepatha, Dhuma, Ekargala, Saniudaya, Rahuudaya, Ketuudaya and Gulikodaya.

Of these, Visha Ghatika, Vishti, Gandanta, Vaidrita, Latta, Ekargala are nithya doshas; Parivesha, Dhuma, Vyatheepatha, Gulika are Upagraha doshas. Shaniudya, Rahuudya, Ketuudya are planetary doshas. The remaining three sthunas are not so well known" but they are also important.

Regarding nithya doshas any treatise on Astrology will give you the method of their calculation. Planetary doshas can be known from almanacs.

The three Sthuna Doshas are Sthuna, Rakta Sthuna and Kantaka Sthuna. These are not very common and they are explained below: -

Kantaka Sthuna: Note the constellation in which the Sun is posited at the time of birth or query time. Count from this asterism till Moola. Note the number. Count the same number from Moola and you will get a constellation. This is Kantaka Sthuna.

Sthuna: Similarly count from the constellation in which Kuja is posited to Moola, you get Sthuna.

Rakta Sthuna: Add up the two numbers and count the number from Moola and you get Rakta Sthuna. If the total exceeds 27, deduct 27 from the same. These are very important for finding out general prosperity.

Nava Doshas are six nithya doshas, gulikodaya and papodaya (Rahu and Saturn). Of course there are differences of opinion regarding this.

Q. 21. What is the purpose of daily yogas found in almanacs? Are we to observe them?

Ans. Undoubtedly you have to take note of them. It is true that they are seldom taken notice of in modern days. They are all necessary for Muhurthas. Auspicious moments are to be looked into for every detail of our actions. Examination of horoscopes in minute detail is not within the reach of all. Prasna too requires other's help. But a study of these Yoga

Kalas is within the reach of all since they are included in almanacs. Dosha Kalas (evil times) can be avoided and good and auspicious times can be selected for doing anything.

Q. 22. Define time of birth.

Ans. Views differ. Some take Bhusparsa (touching the earth) as the birth time. Some consider the time of rupturing of the bag of water and a few others consider the time when the child first cries as birth-time even though there is no Bhusparsa. Satyacharya, the author of Dhruvanadi is quite clear. According to him the horoscope should be cast for the time at which the child falls to the ground as the other two namely, conception and Sirodaya or the appearance of the head, cannot be easily cognised.

Q. 23. Of the books Brihat Jataka, Parasara Hora, Jataka Parijata, Sarwartha Chinthamani and Phala Deepika, which is the most authentic and which should be given preference?

Ans. Parasara Hora is by far the most authoritative. The other works are not by Rishis but by experts in Astrology who were also gifted persons. Each work is valuable in its own way as are different text-books on the same subject, but more readily accessible to us and more easy of interpretation and in that sense, more useful to us. Of all the text-books mentioned, Brihat Jataka is considered more useful from the student's point of view.

Q. 24. What are the characteristics of the celestial body Agastya?

Ans. Agastya which is generally identified with Canopus rises when the Sun is roughly about 7° from Virgo or is about to enter the constellation of Chitta which he generally does in October. Agastya sets when the Sun enters Rohini, which will be the case every year by about May 25th. The time of rising and setting of Agastya varies from place to place and for details reference may be made to Colebrook's comments in Pancha Siddhantika. The results of Agastya are considered only in respect of world events and not in individual horoscopes.

Q. 25. Is the view that Saturn has no Moudhya (combustion) correct?

Ans. Saturn has Moudhya as do the other planets. When he is within 15° forwards or backwards from the Sun, he has Moudhya. But in determining longevity, Saturn's combustion is ignored and no astangata harana (reduction) is made in this account.

Q. 26. What is hyleg?

Ans. Hyleg is a sensitive or a vital point in a horoscope. It is not of much importance in Indian Astrology. According to Ptolemy the sign on the angle of the ascendant from the fifth degree above the horizon to the twenty-fifth degree below it; the eleventh, the tenth and ninth houses, and lastly the seventh house are hylegliacal places. The Sun is hyleg when situated in any one of the above places. If the Sun is not so situated, but the Moon is, then she is hyleg.

Q. 27. Do planets in combustion get Astangata evil?

Ans. Moudhya Dosha of Thara planets (Mars, Mercury, Jupiter, Venus and Saturn) when they are in certain positions in proximity to the Sun, causes evil, technically known as Astangata. Mercury and Sun occupying two different Rasis though in the same house do not cause much harm. In Ayurdaya no harana is made for such Budha. Saravali calls Moudhya planets as Vikala planets. According to it, Vikala planets cause much evil. "A person having Vikala planets will be driven out of his country and home. He will be unclean, will be living in foreign countries, molested by enemies. He will have his wealth taken away by enemies."

It is true that the above evils may occur if Moudhya planets are weak. If they are strong, evils will be minimised. Instead, he will experience some good by his contact with the Sun. Here the Sun must be strong, rule Ishta houses and occupy good places. Nipuna Yoga, for example, is caused by Budha Moudhya. Prasna Marga is silent on this point.

Q. 28. Dasamsa as defined (Article 122) in A Manual of Hindu Astrology is different from that in Varshaphal or The Hindu Progressed, Horoscope (Article 26). Which is correct?

Ans. A closer study and better attention paid to these two books should have solved your difficulty. In the beginning of Chapter III of Varshaphal in which the above quotation occurs it has been categorically stated that with regard to planetary relations in Tajaka we have special relations. The same with regard to aspects (Article 13), also with regard to Balas (Article 15) where it is said: "TheTajaka writers seem to consider two kinds of Balas-one for measuring the relative strength and the weakness of planets for purposes of prediction and the other for determining the lord of the year." So also with regard to Dasavargas in which there are several methods of computing the sub-divisions. The one that is peculiarly adapted to the Tajaka system is given in Varshaphal. The other method is the more general and used in ordinary astrology. So, both are correct.

Q. 29. Define Bhava Chakra.

Ans. Bhava Chakra: RasiChakra shows the position of the planets and Lagna but this does not necessarily indicate the twelve Bhavas for which a Bhava Chakra has to be erected. The rules for the erection of bhava chakra cannot be given here as they are too complicated. Just as there is a point in the eastern horizon which is called the Lagna, there is another point in the Zodiac which is at the zenith at a given moment. This is the Zenith or M.C. The distance from M.C. to Ascendant constitutes a quarter of the Zodiac. The M.C. can be calculated for a given place and time. The origin of the term meridian or mid-heaven of the horpscope implies a space of about 30° bisected by the meridian point. This is exactly what is done in the Indian system and constitutes the tenth house or Bhava of the horoscope. The space between the M.C. and Lagna has to be trisected and the dividing points fixed. The two middle points thus located are the middle points of the 11th and 12th Bhavas. Whereas each Rasi is always 30 degrees each Bhava is not necessarily sp, because the space between M.C. and Lagna often varies according to the latitude of the place for which the horoscope is cast. Lagna Bhava, second Bhava and third Bhava are got by similarly trisecting the distance between the Lagna point and Nadir or the opposite point of M.C. got by adding 180° to the M.C. Thus six Bhavas from 10 to 3 are derived. The other six Bhavas are the ones opposite these Bbavas. Thus all the twelve Bhavas are formed and a chakra which is so formed is called Bhava Cbakra. A detailed exposition of this subject is to be found in A Manual of Hindu Astrology.

CHAPTER - II

Concerning the Bhavas

Q. 30. How do you find out who is the lord of the Bhava when one Bhava is represented by two Rasis?

Ans. Bhava Madhya represents the central point of a Bhava. The lord of the Rasi where the central point falls is the lord of that Bhava.

Q. 31. If all planets, except, say Saturn, are hemmed in between Rahu and Ketu, does it constitute Kalasarpa Yoga?

Ans. By Kalasarpa Yoga is meant the situation of all planets between the two nodes. When Saturn is outside the semicircle forming this yoga, then it implies the cancellation of the yoga.

Q. 32. Is there any truth in the saying that Jupiter, posited in Aquarius, is equivalent to Jupiter in Cancer?

Ans. Brihat Jataka, Chapter 16, verse 26 gives this effect, though Saravali gives bad effects. The former is more authoritative. Many things are beyond our explanation and logic and they should not be rejected on that score.

Q. 33. "For persons born in Scorpio Lagna, Mars is bad and will kill the native if ill-disposed," says Jataka Chandrika. "Mars is not a malefic for persons born in Scorpio" says Parasara. How do you reconcile these?

Ans. Here we have no contradiction. For persons born in Scorpio, Mars is the lord of both 1 and 6. As such he may exercise any one of the powers or both. According to Mantreswara, he will exercise the lordship of 6 since the Moolathrikona for Mars is Aries which is the 6th house. Anyhow, he will exercise his power as the 6th lord if he is disposed. If he happens to be strong well-posited and otherwise favourable, he will exercise his powers as lord of 1 which is always good.

Q. 34. When Saturn falls in Mars' Sapta Vargas and Mars in Saturn's vargas, do they become strong?

Ans. You cannot lay down any hard and fast rule in judging the strength or otherwise of planets when there is an exchange of vargas between two natural malefics. If it is a case of Parivarthana Yoga (interchange of places), this considerably strengthens it. In cases other than a Parivarthana, due weight must be given to their lordship and similar factors. When Mars is a Yogakaraka and Saturn happens to be in Mars' vargas, then Saturn is automatically rendered strong. As to whether such strength expresses itself in good or bad respects depends upon the horoscopic disposition of Saturn though by virtue of Saturn's inherent malefic nature, a measure of evil is bound to predominate.

Q. 35. It is said that if all planets crowd in one half of the Rasi Chakra, the native may not live long.

Ans. There is no authority for such a statement. When all the planets are weak and crowd in one or two Rasis and the birth takes place in inauspicious moments as explained in Brihat Jataka, death may take place. When all the planet are in Mrityu Amsas death may take place.

Q. 36. Several astrologers hold that the 10th house governs father whereas you say in your books that the 9th rules father. Which is correct?

Ans. Whatever may be the views of the several astrologers you refer to regarding the house ruling father, experience has clearly shown that the 9th is the Pithrusthana or house of father. This is further supported by well-known ancient writers such as Mantreswara who observes thus: आचार्यदैवत पितृन् शुभपूर्वभाग्य: meaning that aaharya (preceptor), daivata (deity), pithru (father), are the names for the 9th house. Vaidyanatha, author of the famous Jathaka Parijatha, also corroborates this. My grandfather the late Prof. B. Suryanarain Rao inclines to the same view that 9th indicates father. Apart from these authoritative views take the horoscopes of persons whose fathers are well off in life and you will invariably find the 9th and its lord strongly and beneficially disposed.

Q. 37. What is the effect of the mutual aspect of the two great malefics Saturn and Mars? Do they indicate violence? Does it make any difference if Saturn is the lord of 1?

Ans. No such general rule can be given. It depends on the position and ownership of the aspecting planets. Saravali ascribes the following results.

When Saturn occupies Aries or Scorpio and is aspected by Mars, the native will injure innocent animals, will be a leader of goondas (niffians), will be addicted to drink and women but he will also be famous (Khyatha).

When Saturn occupies Taurus or Libra aspected by Mars, the native will be fond of warlike stories and will be cowardly in the battlefield, and will be a braggart.

When Saturn occupies Gemini or Virgo and is aspected by Mars, he will be obstinate, will be awkward in form and appearance, will be attacked by fits, and will carry others burden.

When Saturn occupies Cancer and is aspected by Mars, be will become rich through royal or divine favour, will be maimed in physique, will have wealth, servants and ornaments and will be fond of bad relations and women.

When Saturn occupies Leo and is aspected by Mars, he will be an itinerant and ungrateful, will be thievish, will frequent hilly places or forests or forts, will be without wife or children.

When Saturn occupies Sagittarius or Pisces and Mars aspects the same, he will be attacked by severe gout, will be despised by people, will live in foreign countries and will be miserly and poor.

When Saturn occupies Capricorn or Aquarius and is aspected by Mars, he will be warlike, will be famous and adventurous and will be a leader of men.

Similarly, when Mars occupies Aries or Scorpio and Saturn aspects the same, he will be weak, will be devoid of followers or relations, will marry another wife.

When Mars occupies Taurus or Libra and Saturn aspects the same, he will be happy, famous, rich, learned and will be a leader of men.

When Mars occupies Gemini or Virgo and is aspected by Saturn, he will be an agriculturist, employed in mining, will be an itinerant, will be an occupant of hilly places and forts, will be poor, dirty and miserable.

When Mars occupies Cancer and is aspected by Saturn, he will be a navigator, poor, beautiful, and engaged in princely trades.

When Mars occupies Leo and is aspected by Saturn, he will be prematurely old, poor, will be living in others' houses, and will be unhappy.

When Mars occupies Sagittarius or Pisces and is aspected by Saturn, he will be ugly, warlike, sinful, a traveller, and bereft of wealth, health and one's Dharma.

When Mars occupies Capricorn or Aquarius- and aspected by Saturn, he will become a king, wealthy but despised by women; will have many children, will be warlike and learned but unhappy.

Q. 38. Is it good to have an evil planet debilitated in a good house? Or, to have an evil planet weakened in a bad house?

Ans. A weak evil planet in a good house or a bad house, wherever he may be, will spoil the house more than a strong evil planet. Here, the general principle to be borne in mind is this. Evil planets, wherever they may be, spoil the house they occupy, the weaker they are the more so it will be.

Q. 39. Is Jupiter's aspect in debilitation good?

Ans. Jupiter is primarily a benefic by nature. Though he is in debilitation. he still retains his benefic nature and his aspect will be good though weak.

Q. 40. Bhavartha Ratnakara says if malefics occupy kendras, good results will happen. Tamil authors say that Saturn in Lagna is bad. How do you explain these contradictory statements?

Ans. It is true that malefics in kendras are good and it is also equally true that malefics in kendras are bad. Malefics in kendras are bad for the Bhavas and good for themselves only. Saturn will be able to do good in everything that pertains to Saturn as a Karaka or as a Bhava lord or as a planet. This will be experienced in his Bhuktis and Dasas, while the house where he is posited will be spoiled and everything connected with the Bhava on which he stands will be unfavourable. If he is in 1, the person's health will be weak, there will be impediments to success etc., and these will be experienced throughout life.

Q. 41. What are the effects of Dhuma, and the other Upagrahas in different Bhavas of a horoscope?

Ans. Dhuma in Lagna, the native will fall in a well; in 2, he will stammer; in 3, his brothers will become lame; in 4, his uncle will be the owner or manager of temple properties; in 5, he will be easily provoked; in 6, cruel animals such as tigers will bite his face; in 7, he will leave his native place as a result of being excommunicated from his caste-or being dismissed from service; in 8, he will receive wounds from weapons; in 9, he will be irreligious; in 10, he will die of lightning; in 11, he will get a new house besides his own native home; in 12, he will leave the house of his birth and wander abroad.

Vyatheepatha in 1 makes the native suffer from skin diseases; in 2, he will become intelligent; in 3, he will be fond of music; in 4, he will earn houses; in 5, he will meet with loss of issues; in 6, he will become a quarrelmonger causing dissensions in family; in 7, he will be poor; in 8, he will be versed in arts; in 9, he will become unlucky; in 10, the native will suffer from burns or incendiarism; in 11, he will be a frequent royal guest; and in 12, he will be an outcaste or expelled servant.

Parivesha in 1, he will die of snake-bite; in 2, he will get treasure troves; in 3, he will become insane; in 4, he will live outside his own house; in 5, he will meet with imprisonment; in 6, he will be a thief in his own house; in 7, he will become one-eyed; in 8, his body will receive hurts from weapons; in 9 , he will not respect his elders or preceptors; in 10, he will be hospitable and charitable; in 11, he will not be able to talk much (want of fluency); and in 12, he will suffer, from chronic diseases.

Indra Chapa in 1, the person will suffer from rheumatic complaints; in 2, he will be deaf; in 3, he will do wicked deeds; in 4, he will misappropriate public money; in 5, he will become timid and well versed in Mantra Sastras; in 6, he will often meet with reverses from his enemies; in 7, he will lose one of his limbs in his body and he will lose his wife; in 8, he will wander baffled in all his ambitions; in 9, he will die as a result of his own son or imprisonment; in 10, he will eat quickly and be a poor man; in 11, he will be valorous and fond of hunting; and in 12, he will be banished as a result of royal displeasure.

Upa Ketu in 1, the native will be bald in his forehead; in 2, he will be weak and talk through the nose; in 3, he will talk through the nose and he will talk little and he will be afraid of others' words; in 4, he will dress neatly and decorate himself decently; in 5, he will suffer from complicated diseases; in 6, he will become stone-blind and die in others' houses due to severe lung diseases; in 7, he will die as a result of thieving or will commit suicide; in 8, he will die by consuming poison; in 9, he will be brave and heroic in actions and in the end he will meet with an unnatural death; in 10, he will fall from a tree or a tree fall on him; in 11, he will get treasure; and in 12, he will have no happiness when asleep and he will meet with heavy losses and miseries.

When do these effects come to pass? The answer is in the Dasa or Bhukti periods of lords wherein these are posited or in the periods of planets that are associated with or aspected by these Upagrahas. The effects will be effective in most cases. These results are only general.

Q. 42. Is a natural malefic, like Saturn, evil or good when exalted or in own house?

Ans. Even a natural malefic becomes benefic if in his own or exaltation house. Though Saturn in 4 is bad for mother, happiness, education etc., normally, if he is exalted or in his own place he is not bad. But to become fully benefic he must combine with, say Venus or be aspected by Jupiter for a malefic can become a Yogakaraka but cannot become a full benefic. This is the result in practical experience. For instance, such a man with Saturn in 4 may pass and get degrees but may not have a brilliant academic career without any failures at all. For Aries Lagna, Saturn in Taurus, the house immediately after debilitation and the house of his very intimate friend will give position and income as lord of 10 and 11 in 2, more especially if that lord Venus is strong or if there is also the aspect of Jupiter. But as a natural malefic, he will certainly cause some wasteful expenditure and some trouble in the family like loss of children.

Q. 43. How can we determine the fortune of an individual during war-time?

Ans. Individual destiny is not altered by war. Those who die in war along with others, as in earthquakes or floods must have indications of such death in groups. For, are we not aware of the miraculous providential escape of some from the debris of an earthquake where many perished? There are others who prosper even in times of famine while yet others perish even in times of plenty. A lieutenant or a commander having good longevity will survive any dangers he may be exposed to while fighting a battle. There is a design in our life and it works its way irrespective of our noticing it.

Q. 44. (a) What planetary combinations make one an expert in different languages? Are there any such thing as Aryan and non-Aryan languages?

(b) What influences make one an expert astrologer and astr onomer such as B. Suryanarain Rao was?

(c) Is a knowledge of thought-reading and mesmerism necessary for being a successful predictor?

Ans. (a) A careful perusal of standard astrological books in Sanskrit reveals no information as to what combinations make one well versed in different languages. At the time when the Maharshis - composed astrological treatises, Sanskrit occupied such a pre-eminent place that everyone aspired to become a scholar in it. Sanskrit was the repository of all knowledge, spiritual and secular and consequently acquaintance with or proficiency in other languages was, not of much importance in those days. Hence, the absence of combinations for linguistic proficiency.

However, examination of a large number of horoscopes reveal that Jupiter must be the karaka for the language. If he is in Lagna or aspects the 9th house, one will know several languages. The second house indicates speech. If Ketu is in the 2nd or the lord of the 2nd happens to see the 2nd then the native will become well versed in a number of languages. The second house and Jupiter are the most important factors for judging linguistic capabilities.

(b) Jupiter and Mercury well placed in a kendra or kona make one a capable astrologer. This is well illustrated in the horoscope of late Prof. B. Suryanarain Rao. The Sun, the 4th lord, and Mercury, the 2nd and 5th lord, are placed in the 10th with Jupiter. This is a unique combination. There are different grades of astrologers. Alan Leo was no doubt a good writer but he has hardly any predictions to his credit whereas Prof. B. Suryanarain Rao was not only an intellectual giant but a correct predictor. Reference to standard works will reveal any number of combinations but I give herewith a few important ones which make one a good astrologer and astronomer.

(1) Mercury in a kendra, Venus in the 2nd and another benefic in the 3rd makes one an expert astrologer; (2) if Jupiter owning the 2nd house becomes the most powerful planet and Venus is exalted, a famous astrologer is born; (3) if Mars is fortified in the 2nd and conjoins the Moon and Mercury or if Mercury is in a kendra with the Moon and Mars, one becomes a good mathematician; (4) if Mercury is the lord of the 2nd, and Jupiter is in a kendra, and Venus is exalted, the native becomes an expert mathematician; (5) if lord of the 2nd Mercury be in exaltation, Jupiter be in Lagna and Saturn be in the 8th, one becomes an expert in mathematics.

(c) Thought-reading and mesmerism belong to the category of what is called Kshudra or inferior or base knowledge. Consequently, they do not form part of the divine knowledge of astrology. On the contrary the power of prediction depends to a large extent on the development of what is called intuition. This can be acquired by leading a simple, moral and disciplined life free from the vices of modern civilization and by practising certain principles of conduct laid down in the Sastras. Thus you will see that the so-called thought-reading and hypnotism have nothing to do with astrology proper and that they are only adventitious growths which should be removed from time to time.

Q. 45. According to Brihat Jataka the Kendra (quadrangular) aspects of the Sun and the Moon are bad. Does it refer to Cancer and Leo subjects?

Ans. Brihat Jataka gives the general rule. The kendra aspects of the Sun and the Moon are bad, and it refers to persons born in all Rasis However, persons born in Cancer and Leo will have slightly better results caused by lordship.

Q. 46. How do you find out whether two men will become friends?

Ans. Examine the Lagnas or Chandra Lagnas of the two horoscopes. If they are not in shashtashtama (6th and 8th) positions, they will be friends; if the lords of the Rasis above referred to are in Adhimitra positions, they will become friends.

Q. 47. In Bhavartha Ratnakara, it is stated that "all such Bhavas whose lords are in conjunction with the respective karakas become strong". What would be the effect if karakas are themselves the lord of the Karaka Bhavas, for example for Aquarius Lagna the third house being Aries, lord of 3 and the karaka of the 3rd Bhava would be Mars. If he is posited in Lagna, will the 3rd Bhava gain strength?

Ans. It is stated that when a karaka occupies his own Bhava, the Bhava (house) and the karaka (indicator) become unfavourable. If Venus, the karaka of 7 is in 7, Venus and the 7th house become unfavourable. Similarly Moon in 4, Sun in 9, Mars in 3, Mercury in 4, Jupiter in 5 are unfavourable. Saturn alone is excepted. Saturn in the 8 confers long life.

Bhavartha Ratnakara states that those Bhavas whose lords are in conjunction with the respective karakas become strong. Suppose the ascendant is Leo, the karaka of Lagna is the Sun. The third house is Libra. The karaka of 3 is Mars. If the lord of 3, viz., Venus is in conjunction with Mars, the third house becomes strong. Suppose Aquarius is Lagna and the lord of the 3rd house also is posited in 3. In that case, the 3rd house becomes favourable. If the lord of the 3rd house and karaka of the 3rd house is in Lagna, the third Bhava does not gain strength because of the above rule. However, he (Mars) will have Kendra strength.

Q. 48. How do you reconcile the statements:

(a) A person will be fortunate in respect of that Bhava whose karaka is situated in the 12th house from Lagna.

(b) planets in 6, 8 and 12 are generally unfavourable?

Ans. (a) For instance for a Simha Lagna horoscope, if Mars the karaka of 3 is in Cancer, the native will be fortunate in brothers. This applies to karakas and the Bhava which the karaka represents.

(b) the second is a general statement affecting planets as such and applies only to their lordships (Bhavadhipathya). In the same example, Mars is lord of 4 and posited in 12-Cancer. All the 4th house prospects are shut out to him.

Q. 49. What is the effect and strength of planets that are in debilitation in Rasi but exalted in Navamsa?

Ans. Though Parasara is of the opinion that planets in exaltation but in debilitated Navamsa are not favourable while those in exalted Navamsa and Neecha Rasi do good, we cannot accept it. Navamsa strength is one of the sources of strength and only from balavrinda (sum total of strength) can we know the correct strength and from this; we have to give the effects. In the stanza referred to, the author has only given the comparative importance of Navamsa in Dasa Vargas.

Q. 50. What is Vargottama Navamsa?

Ans. When the Rasi and Navamsa Rasi of planets or Bhavas happen to bear the same Rasi, we have Vargottama.

Q. 51. Define hemming in between evil planets. Will it be papamadhyasthithi if a planet is posited midway between two evil planets, all the three planets occupying one and the same sign or two Rasis, or is it necessary that three different houses should be involved for hemming? Is there any difference in effect between these?

Ans. The term 'papamadhyasthithi' means situated between evil planets. This necessarily applies whether it takes place in a single sign or in two or three signs. But there is a difference in their practical application. The term is generally held to denote the state when a planet in one sign is beseiged by evil planets from both the adjacent signs. When this occurs in a single sign itself, this is classed in Hindu Astrology as conjunction which is considered more powerful than 'hemming'. When only two signs are involved, it is neither hemming nor conjunction but is considered as Dwirdwadasa.

Q. 52. In Jataka Parijata, it is stated that Jupiter in Scorpio, Aries and Sagittarius is very powerful. There is also the view that "Vrischika (Scorpio), an insect sign" is unfavourable for Jupiter. How do you reconcile these contradictions?

Ans. The reference in the former is to natal astrology and in the latter, to mundane events. Jupiter is certainly powerful in Sagittarius, Pisces and Scorpio for purpose of conserving vital energy and conferring long life. Jupiter in Scorpio, at the same time, can pervert one's character, unless it happens to be the 9th or 10th house. The two apparently contrary attributes relate to different departments of life.

Q, 53. What is the result if a debilitated and an exalted planet are in one house?

Ans. There will be neutralisation of effects, when two such planets combine in one house. If the exalted planet is stronger by proportion, the effect of the exalted planet will prevail.

Q. 54. How do you predict if a person will be deceived by (a) friends, (b) enemies, (c) relations,(d) females and (e) foreigners?

Ans. If both the 6th and 12th houses and their lords are weak and joined or aspected by friendly planets, the native will be deceived by his friends. In the same way, if the said planets are in conjunction with inimical planets, planets occupying own vargas and Saturn and Rahu, the native will be dec ived by his enemies, relatives and foreigners respectively. Sex is determined by the position of the said planets in male or female signs and amsas respectively.

Q. 55. The author of Susloka Satakam says: "Persons born in Kali Yuga will suffer from all the evil results, if planets indicate full bad results and the person will enjoy 1/4th of the good results if planets indicate full good results." How far is this correct?

Ans. Such statements cannot be accepted on their face value. They are relatively true. All astrological principles, that are applicable in Kali Yuga, have their sanction in Parasara's writings. Therefore, there is no question of a man enjoying a part of the good indications and the sum total of the evil indications of the horoscope. The results-good, indifferent or bad of one's past karma, which a horoscope indicates, can be modified or augmented by deeds in this life. This is the commonsense point of view. In Yuga Dharma, it is stated that the ratio of good and bad karma one does in Kali Yuga is 1: 4 and what the author of Susloka Satakas says is only a reflection of the views of Yuga Dharma.

Q. 56. Explain the terms Pachaka, Karaka, Bhodaka and Vedaka.

Ans. The term "Pachaka" implies fruitless or giving up result. Karaka implies giving the results slowly. Bhodaka implies giving the results quickly. Vedaka means causing obstruction to the free-play of the results. The Sun is a Pachaka by nature. Moon is a Bhodaka by nature. Sun is also a Karaka by nature and Moon is also a Bhodaka by nature. Planets by their positions from one another become Pachaka or Karaka or Bhodaka or Vedaka. More details can be found from Parasara Hora and Sarwartha Chinthamani.

Q. 57. Do slow-moving planets like Saturn, Jupiter and Rahu show their Kshetra (house) effects more than their effects in sign (Asraya Phala)?

Ans. Planets derive their strength either for good or bad by their situation in signs and by their position in the Kshetras (houses). If they are in their favourable signs and houses, good alone will follow and the native will experience them. If they are in unfavourable signs but in favourable houses, there will be a little good but that little will be enjoyed by the person. If they are in favourable signs but in unfavourable houses as 6, 8, or 12, there will be potential strength for good in the horoscope but the native/will not enjoy it. If both are unfavourable, there will be no strength for good and the native will not experience anything. This idea is beautifully expressed in Prasna Marga. As slow-moving planets stay longer in various signs the effects will be longer felt. The effects of signs, how long and what they are, are to be ascertained by the transit of planets through the various Kakshyas that compose a Rasi. For details reference may be made to Prasna Marga (Chapter 32, 23rd verse) or Ashtakavarga System of Prediction.

Q. 58. What is the value of Dhana Saham in judging a horoscope?

Ans. Generally it is not applied in reading a horoscope according to Parasara. It is used to ascertain "wealth" when "Varshaphala" is read according to Tajaka system. It can also be used in horary astrology when examined according to the principles of the same system.

Q. 59. Saturn is a malefic planet, but he becomes a benefic by owning kendras. If so, are his aspects also benefic? Is the term "aspected by benefics". occurring in the texts applicable to "Saturn" and such evil planets?

Ans. Saturn is always an evil planet but may be malefic or benefic by ownership. We can classify planets into four kinds: subha and subha phalada-good and favourable; subha and papa phalada-good and unfavourable; papa and subha phalada-evil and favourable; and papa and papa phalada-evil and unfavourable. Whenever you find "aspected by benefics" we have to take "good or subha planets". In the expression "benefic aspects" it means only aspects by natural benefics such as Jupiter and Venus.

Q. 60. Is the aspect of New Moon or Weak Moon and badly associated Mercury inauspicious?

Ans. Weak Moon and badly associated Mercury are considered malefics. According to Bhattotpala, the Moon is weak from the 8th lunar day of the dark half to the 8th of the bright half.

In regard to longevity determination, the Moon is held to be weak only from the 13th day of the dark half to the end of new Moon. In Skanda Hora it is stated that the Moon is weak only on the 14th or 15th lunar days of the dark half and not always. When Mercury is associated with weak Moon or Sun or Mars or Saturn, he becomes a malefic. Weak Moon is also malefic. The Sun is a malefic. Mars is a malefic because of his thamasaic qualities. Saturn is a malefic because of his grief-causing qualities. Mercury's malefic nature is not caused by any one of the above reasons but caused by 'yoga'- only. As such Skanda Hora wants us to take him only as a non-subha (non-benefic) and not as papa (malefic). Therefore, the aspect of a badly associated Mercury will bring in neither malefic nor benefic effects.

Q. 61. What is the effect of planets in Bhava Sandhis?

Ans. In the middle of the Bhava, it gives fully the results accruing from that Bhava in the respective Dasas. As it recedes or proceeds, the effects decrease or increase proportionately. If a planet is at the end of the 6th Bhava, the results of the 6th house will be, least seen in the Dasa of the planet.

Q. 62. Several Lagnas have been mentioned in different astrological treatises. What are their uses?

Ans. Different authors have given different kinds of Lagna. The earliest works, Jaimini Sutras and Parasara Hora, mention Aroodha Lagna, Hora Lagna, Bhava Lagna etc. Later writers emphasize (1) Ascendant or Time of Birth and (2) Chandra Lagna. In Prasna Marga, we have Udaya Lagna (time of query) and Aroodha.

All these can be utilised for prediction. Except the last two, all the rest can be made use of in horoscopy. Horoscopy can be used for reading past, present and future lives. Past lives can be read better with the Lagnas mentioned in Jaimini Sutras. Present life can be studied by a comparative study of Prasna Lagnas (Aroodhs and Udaya Lagna) and Chandra Lagna and the time of birth. Future life can be better understood by Janma Lagna and Chandra Lagna. Next life (life after death) can be studied by Ravi Lagna and Chandra Lagna.

The classification may seem to be arbitrary but it has to be borne in mind that all these can be used for reading our lives past, present and future. The reason for giving out so many kinds of Lagnas is that the subject is so vast that it becomes very difficult to affirm or negate a fact with the help of a single method. The question must be touched in as many ways as possible.Herein lies the greatness of Hindu astrology. Varaha Mihira wants us to examine the questions in as many ways as possible in his chapter on Nashta Jataka. If there is agreement we can take it as correct, not otherwise. There may be a general rule and there may be many exceptions. In the ordinary texts, we study only general rules. An astrologer may be very learned and still may not be aware of the exceptions. As such he has to approach the question very cautiously through various ways. Then only can he h t at the right solution.

In Prasna or Horary, besides the Lagnas mentioned above, we make use of Nimitha, Chesta, Numbers, Sakuna and many others.

Q. 63. Is there any injunction that horoscopes of new-born children are to be cast after a particular age?

Ans. There are no such injunctions. But Parasara is of the opinion that the longevity of a child cannot be guaged before it completes its 12th year even if there are no Balarishta Yogas. Parents are primarily responsible for the bringing up of children and their Karmas, viz., actions, past and present, go a long way in preserving their lives. Death may happen in two ways-Kala Mrityu (once in one's life) and Akala Mrityu (in every year): It is said that Akala Mrityu (accidents) can be got over by suitable remedial measures, while Kala Mrityu (final death) cannot be avoided. Upagrahas determine the nature and time of Akala Mrityu. Children are not expected to perform prayaschittas (penances) before they come of age. Hence it is clear that the actions of parents are responsible for the longevity of children.

Again it is said that Yogas in a horoscope are ineffective till the 12th year and Dasas till the 16th year. This could be the basis of the statement.

Q. 64. Some say that lords of Dusthanas must be in their own houses. Others say that they must be weak and as such must not be in swakshetras. Which is correct?

Ans. According to the first, the evil lords in their own houses safeguard the interest of the evil houses as a result evils are minimised. According to the second view, planets in their. own houses get strength and cause miseries. Varaha Mihira is of the opinion that malefics if weak will cause more miseries, while a strong malefic will not cause evils. Here only one aspect of strength is taken into consideration. In such cases Bala Pinda must be prepared and Ishta Phala and Anishta Bala worked out, as per Graha and Bhava Balas.

In Vipareeta Raja Yoga, lords of 6, 8 and 12 exchange places. This is only a special yoga and must not be mixed up with the simple exchange of the lord of 6 and 8, 8 and 12 or 6 and 12. Effects are different.

Q. 65. Why are the lords of any two opposite signs enemies, i.e., the lord of Aries, Mars is inimical to Venus the lord of Libra? How can you explain this scientifically?

Ans. The assumption that Mars is the enemy of Venus is wrong. Venus and Mars are neutral to each other. But the principle stated is correct as regards the other planets. The Moon has no enemies. Mercury is inimical to Jupiter, and the Moon and the Sun are enemies to Saturn. It is a necessary consequence of the principle of polarity which is behind the scheme of planetary lordship. This has been explained in an article in the January 1941 issue of The Astrological Magazine. The story goes that the Sun and the Moon owned the entire Zodiac originally between themselves and then each gave to the other planets one sign in the order of their orbits; in that Mercury first got one sign from the Moon (Gemini) and another from the Sun (Virgo). Next came Venus who got Taurus and Libra from each; then Mars, then Jupiter, then Saturn. This story is based on the scientific truth that polarity or opposition is behind this arrangement. The ownership of the 12 signs is distributed in 3 sets of polar opposites. The Sun and the Moon owning Cancer and Leo are balanced by Saturn owning the opposite signs of Capricorn and Aquarius. Next comes Mercury which rules Gemini and Virgo and is balanced by Jupiter owning Sagittarius and Pisces and then the opposition of Venus, lord of Taurus and Libra by Mars ruling Aries and Scorpio follows. It is a misnomer to call this balancing or opposition as enmity though this principle when translated into the plane of human action sometimes operates as enmity and to that extent only is correct. The first house indicates the native and the seventh his wife; their respective lords also stand for the same, but the husband cannot be considered an enemy of his wife. In fact, this opposition is to be considered as complementary in this connection.

Q. 66. According to Saravali (9th chapter, verses 32 and 33) if Jupiter does not aspect Lagna or the Moon or the Sun and the Moon are together, or the Sun and the Moon are associated with powerful malefics, the birth is illegitimate. In actual practice it is found that even in cases where Jupiter does not aspect Lagna or the Moon the mother is of unquestionable chastity. Please explain.

Ans. The above verses are very general statements and there are many (48) exceptions noted by the venerable Sounaka Rishi in his conversation with Brihaspati. They are as follows:

(a) When ascendant or the Moon is in Guru (Jupiter) Kshetra, or Drekkana, or Navamsa or they are associated with Jupiter, he cannot be considered a jara putra or as born of a prostitute. (b) When the vargas of Lagna or the Moon have no malefic influence, (c) When the vargas of the lord of 9 preponderate in Lagna Varga, (d) When the Moon is in Venusian Varga and Lagna in Venus Navamsa, (e) When a strong Jupiter without having the lordship of 8 aspects 9, (f) When the 10th house from the Moon is aspected by Jupiter, (g) When the lord of 11 is Venus and is posited between Jupiter and the Moon, (h) When the 9th house from the Moon is occupied by Mercury and Venus, (i) When the 10th house from the Moon is aspected by the Sun posited in fixed houses, (j) When the Moon has Vargottamamsa and association with the lord of 10 from himself, (k) When the Moon is in a benefic house not associated with or aspected by malefics, (l) When the Moon is in a Subha Kendra, free from the aspect of malefics, (m) When Venus occupies the first or 2nd Navamsa of Cancer, (n) When Venus strongly aspected by the Sun occupies the 12th house from the Moon, (o) When the Moon is in exalted Rasi orNavamsa, (p) When the Moon is in his own house free from the aspect of the lord of 12 (from the Moon), (q) When the Moon is in the first Drekkana of Gemini, 2nd Drekkana of Libra, or 3rd Drekkana of Aquarius, (r) When the Moon occupies Gemini, Libra or Aquarius Navamsa, (s) When the Mandala Sphuta of the Moon is in Guru Kshetra, or Drekkanas, (t) When the Sphuta got by subtracting Chandra Sphuta from Ravi Sphuta has no Guru Shadvarga, (u) If a malefic joins the Moon and the former owns the 7th house from him (the Moon), (v) If Jupiter, posited in Saturn's Trimsamsa ,or associated with Ketu or if he owns the 8th house from the Moon does not aspect Lagna or the Moon, (w) Vhen Jupiter happens to be a temporary friend of the Moon and lord of I and at the same time ocupies Lagna or the Moon Navamsa, (x) When the lord of 5 from the Moon is exalted and aspects the Moon, (y) When a temporary friend of the Moon aspected by Jupiter aspects the Moon.

These yogas have been taken from Brihat Sounaka Hora.

Q. 67. Which planets rule the following: Paternal and maternal uncles, father-in-law and mother-in-law, brother-in-law and sister-in-law from the wife's side, sister-in-law from the paternal side and daughter-in-law?

Ans. The 7th or 11th house governs paternal uncles. The 2nd or 6th house governs maternal uncles. The 3rd house represents father-in-law, the 10th house represents mother-in-law, the 5th and 9th houses represent respectively brother and sister-in-law from wife's side, the 5th and the 1st house represents sister-in-law from paternal side. The 11th house represents daughter-in-law.

Q. 68. How does Mandi determine the maraka planet?

Ans. Mandi is an indicator of maraka. Ascertain the asterism occupied by Mandi at the time of a person's birth. The Dasa of Gulika is reckoned from this star. The maraka planet will be one among the lords of the Rasi and Navamsa occupied by Mandi as well as the planet in conjunction with Mandi.

Q. 69. What is meant by the lord of the 22nd Drekkana?

Ans. Each Rasi is divided into three equal parts. The lord of each part so divided is the lord of that sign, the 5th and 9th signs from it respectively. The Lagna will be in some Drekkana. Count 22 Drekkanas from that. The lord of the Drekkana so arrived at is the lord of 22nd Drekkana. He will be generally the lord of the 1st Drekkana of the 8th house.

Q. 70. Why is the Navamsa Chakra considered as being of equal importance to Rasi in the matter of prediction?

Ans. In Rasi Chakra, planets are placed according to their astronomical positions in the Zodiac. In the Navamsa chart, which is considered to be second in importance only to the Rasi Chakra, the planets are arranged according to the subdivisions in which they are found and named in the order of signs beginning from Aries. This is familiar to all students. Beyond giving the positions of the planets and Lagna correct to 3⅓ degrees, an independent chart is prepared and considered along with Rasi Kundali. No doubt the positions in the Navamsa chart are imaginary if their relative positions alone are taken into account. But we have to proceed on the assumption that the seers who propounded the science of astrology knew more about it than we do. They found that with astronomical accuracy, symbolism also played a great part and attributed equal importance to both. The Rasi Kundali is an astronomical chart and Navamsa Chakra is a symbolical chart.

Q. 71. (a) Which planets, signs and Bhavas represent sports-football, hockey, cricket, indoor games etc.?

(b) What are the ruling planets for bus drivers, conductors and railway drivers?

Ans. (a) Unfortunately our great Rishis did not specifically touch upon these. Even the Greek astrologers make no mention of these. Hence we have to use our own intelligence and find out appropriate planets and houses suiting the present day requirements from the broad outlines given by them. Mercury indicates sports. The third house governs games indicating valour. Hence Budha Varga (sub-divisions held by Mercury) if strong in the third house or Mercury with more 3rd house vargas, indicates that the native is interested in sports. Sports may pertain to water, land, or air and these have to be distinguished from the nature of the house. Western astrologers consider that Rahu governs sports and it may be accepted for what it is worth.

(b) The 4th house, the lord of 4 and Venus govern conveyances. Mars in the 4th indicates motor cars, or Mars connected with Venus or the 4th house-lord indicates the same. The owner of a motor car can be known when the 4th house or the lord of 4 or Venus is connected with Mars. The 5th and the 11th houses also can be taken. A bus driver need not necessarily be the owner of a bus. Hence the 10th house of the native should have some connection with planets mentioned above.

Q. 72. How do you reconcile the following statements: Malefics and benefics in the 11ᵗʰ produce good; mutual malefic combinations such as Saturn and Mars give bad results?

Ans. There is no contradiction between the above two statements. Mutual conjunction of natural malefics would be harmful provided they occur in certain specific houses such as Lagna, 5ᵗʰ, 9ᵗʰ and so on. The 11ᵗʰ is an exception. Likewise, the presence of benefics in the 11ᵗʰ is equally favourable. Though, in theory, no evil results can happen, in actual practice, benefics are found to lose some of their strength for good by virtue of such evil association-the adverse effects being felt in respect of such Bhavas owned by the benefics.

Q. 73. Western Astrology regards 'opposition' as evil, but in Indian astrology opposition is not always evil. What are the results of the mutual aspects of Jupiter and Mars with reference to Makara (Capricorn) and Kataka (Cancer)?

Ans. The Western school considers the opposition aspects as generally evil, while the Indian school of astrology considers opposition as both good and bad according to the nature of the planets in aspect.

Saravali describes the effects of the aspect of Mars and Jupiter when they are in Capricorn and Cancer respectively thus: "The native will be handsome, will have the qualities and position of a king; will begin things very carefully; will live long; and will be affectionate towards his relatives; will have a young handsome wife; will be rich; will wear ornaments in his body; will be learned; will be valorous, and will have wounds in his body."

Q. 74. How do you determine the winner in planetary war (Graha Yuddha)?

Ans. Two planets are said to be in war when they are in conjunction and the distance between them is less than a day.

All the planets (Taragrahas) excepting the Sun and the Moon can enter into the fight. The victor is the one whose longitude is less.

Q. 75. (a) What are the exaltation places of Rahu and Ketu?

(b) Does Rahu in the constellations of Krittika, Uttara and Uttarashadha intensify the bad effect?

(c) When does Rahu become a Kodanda Rahu?

Ans. (a) Parasara Hora is of the opinion that Taurus and Scorpio are the exaltation (uchcha) Rasis of Rahu and Ketu respectively. Saravali also accepts this view while minor authorities as Jataka Parijata, Jyotisthatwa, Bhavakutuhala etc., consider that Gemini is the exaltation Rasi for Rahu and Sagittarius for Ketu. The first view has to be accepted as being more authoritative.

(b) This is to be applied only for the Gochara or transit effects of planets. For details Brihat Samhita may be referred to.

(c) Rahu becomes Kodanda when he occupies Dhanus (Sagittarius).

Q. 76. Should predictions be based on Rasi Chakra (sign chart) or Bhava Chakra (house chart)?

Ans. Bhava Chakra has to be followed unless otherwise stated in the text. For example, in Ashtaka Varga, Rasi Chakra has to be followed. All yogas can be classified under 7 heads, and we will see that some yogas are based on Rasi and some on Bhava, and we have to make a careful distinction between the two. Sakata and Kesari Yogas are to be read from Bhavas only according to Laghu Jataka Sarvaswa, Chapter III. In reading the effects of planets from position, both should be taken into consideration, viz.: Bhava Phala and Asraya Phala (effects from Rasis).

Q. 77. What are the different kinds of Arudhas?

Ans. Jaimini emphasizes 12 Arudhas: LagnaArudha, Dhanarudha, Vikramarudha etc., one for each Bhava. Arudhas are to be determined as follows:

Note where the lord of the ascendant stands and count as many signs from this Rasi as the ascendant lord is removed from the ascendant. The Rasi so got is Arudha or Pada or Lagna Arudha. Similarly note where the lord of 2 is from the 2nd house and the number of Rasis passed by him. Calculate the same number from the Rasi occupied by the lord of 2. The Rasi so got is Dhana Arudha.

In the same way work for other 'houses' and we get Vikrama Arudha (3rd), Matru Arudha (4th), Santana Arudha (5th), Vyadhi Arudha (6th), Bharya Arudha (7th), Niryana Arudha (8th), Bhagya Arudha (9th), Karma Arudha (10th), Labharudha: (11th) and Upapada or Vyaya Arudha (12th).

Q. 78. Are the neecha or oocha positions of planets determined with reference to their sign or house position?

Ans. Uchha (exaltation) and Neecha (debilitation) are determined only with reference to Rasis (signs) and not Bhavas (houses).

Q. 79. It is said that (a) debilitation for evil planets is good if they own bad houses;

(b) evil planets in kona (trine) or kendra (angle) cause harm to the houses they occupy;

(c) vakra (retrograde) for evil planets is bad. How far are these statements true?

Ans. None of the above statements are absolutely correct. Neechathwa (debilitation) for evil planets if they own dusthanas (malefic places) is not good. Suppose the lord of 8 is debilitated in a horoscope, he cannot do any good. On the contrary, if he is strong, in the course of his Dasa, he will free the native from debts, enemies and poverty. In Horary Astrology (Prasna), however, the above-mentioned statement is only partially true. When the lord of 6, viz., thief, is debilitated and the lord of 1 is stronger, the thief will be caught and the articles lost will be recovered. In natal horoscopes, if the lord of 6, viz., enemy is debilitated, the native will be more exposed to sickness than otherwise.

(b) Evil planets in konas (trines) or kendras (angles) spoil the houses they occupy. Evil planets, wherever they are posited, spoil the houses of occupation. If they occupy 6, enemies increase, if they are in 8 lives is in jeopardy, if they occupy 12, expenses increase. But, when they are in 5 (kona, kendra or upachaya), they gain strength and they are able to confer results beneficial to their nature in their respective Dasa periods.

(c) Vakra (retrograde) planets if they are evil ones, do only evil. This also requires modification. Vakra planets, if they are strong, own good houses and occupy favoutable places do only good in their Dasa periods.

Q. 80. How can you predict previous karma?

Ans. The cumulative effect of previous karma is the present birth. The birth chart indicates the previous sins and merits through planets. When the planets are weak and occupy bad positions, we can conclude that we have committed more sins than merits. If some planets are favourable, we can say we have done more meritorious work. In Prasna (Horary), the 9th house is analysed taking it as Lagna, i.e., 9th House-Karma Swarupa, 10-Karma Dhana, 11-Karma Sahaya, 12-Karma Adhikarana, I-Karma Bhutha Vasthu, 2-Karma Nasa Karana, 3-Karma Sahachari, 4-Karmayus, 5-Karma Bhagya, 6-Karma Vyapara, 7-Karma Labha and 8 is Karma Vyaya.

Q. 81. (a) What is the result of Herschel being in Lagna and Neptune in the 8th house?

(b) Are they benefics or malefics?

(c) Other particulars about them.

Ans. Herschel in Lagna-strong love of freedom and hatred of control, wilfulness in all actions, originality and new ideas; skill in occupations connected with electricity or radio. Nervous disorders, colds, restlessness and haughtiness are some of the faults. Neptune in the 8th-fluctuation in financial prospects, marriage with dowry, money from unexpected sources, losses due to fraud, fits and swoons.

(b) Both are bad planets.

(c) They are not included in Hindu Astrology as even their influences are comprehended by the seven important planets.

Q. 82. When does Venus get moudhya or combust? For example, if Venus is 96 degrees and the Sun is 91 degrees, is the former combust? Does Venus get cancellation of combustion if he owns the Ascendant?

Ans. Venus becomes combust when he is within 7° from the Sun on either side. Yes, Moudhya effects will happen even if Venus is Ascendant lord. Suppose Gemini is Lagna and Mercury has moudhya, then the native will be moving in rural parts insignificant in name but at the same time will feel no financial troubles. This is the effect given to Moodha Mercury by some astrologers. But he will be educated.

Q. 83. In predictions, combination, aspect and position, etc., of Amsa, which are imaginary factors are also given consideration like Rasi (which is actual). Why?

Ans. This is usually a stumbling block for everybody in the beginning of the study of astrology but easily solved as one progresses in the study.

Q. 84. How do you predict a person will be deaf and dumb?

Ans. The 11th house governs the left ear. The third house governs the right ear. Evil planets, weak and afflicted in these houses, cause deafness. Karaka for 'sound' is Saturn. The 2nd house when afflicted causes dislocation of speech organs. Karaka for speech is Venus.

Q. 85. How to know whether one will get financial assistance from his friends?

Ans. Various combinations are given in the texts. But it is better to remember and apply general principles. The eleventh Bhava is the one relating to friends. If the lord of Lagna or the 2nd Bhava conjoins, aspects or receives aspects from lord of 11 or the two lords are in mutual reception, financial help from friends can be expected.

Q. 86. What Grahas are the karakas of Economics, Politics, Botany, Zoology and Psychology?

Ans. Economics-Venus and his signs; Politics-Jupiter and the Sun and Sagittarius and Leo; Botany-Venus and Taurus; Zoology-the Moon, the Sun and Mars, and Cancer, Leo and Scorpio; Psychology- the Sun and Leo.

Q. 87. Can educational qualifications be determined?

Ans. The 4th house indicates education. The 5th house denotes mental advancement. The 2nd house denotes vocal powers. Hence the three houses may be examined in detail. Regarding planets, the Sun indicates philosophy, Moon-medicine, Mars-surgery and agriculture, Mercury-mathematics, Jupiter-literature and aerial sciences, Venus-plant life, and Saturn-history and politics. From these, we can study the other sciences also.

Q. 88. How do you predict whether one will be successful in occult sciences?

Ans. Saturn in 4 or 5 brings success in occult sciences. Venus in 10 or in 2 aspected by the Moon may bring in success. Jupiter in 9 aspected by Saturn makes one learned in Mantra Sastra. Venus in 12, the Sun and Mercury in 11 for Gemini Lagna will bring in success as a partial adept in the science.

Q. 89. How do you predict the number of children?

Ans. There are several methods in vogue which enable us to predict the number of children. In the matter of prediction, the mere application of astrological principles will be of no avail unless the astrologer brings to bear upon the prediction what is called intuition. Any ordinary text-book on astrology will give you the methods for the determination of the number of children. Before attempting the number of children, you should ascertain whether the male's horoscope indicates virility or otherwise and whether he is capable of procreation. In spite of the existence of other favourable factors childlessness may result, if in the horoscope of a woman, the Moon occupies the 3rd, 6th and 11th houses. In the case of a male fitness to procreate and his virile power are ascertained through the Sun, while the fertility of the woman is ascertained through Mars and the Moon. Add together the longitudes of the Sun, Venus and Jupiter in the male horoscope. If the resulting figure diminished by the number of complete circles of 360 degrees falls in a male sign or constellation, then it denotes virility to produce offspring. In the case of a female add together the longitudes of the Moon, Mars and Jupiter. If the resulting-figure diminished by complete circles of 360 degrees falls in a female constellation or sign, then it indicates the woman's strength of fecundity. The following method is also popular: Omit the signs and convert the degrees etc., of the 5th Bhava into minutes. Ascertain the Drigbala (aspect strength) of the different planets on the fifth house. Multiply the minutes by the sum of the Drigbala and take one sixtieth of this product and divide it by 200. The result will indicate the number of issues one will have. By a similar process the children to be lost may be ascertained with the help of the strength of malefic aspects cast on the 5th house. If the lord of the 5th house be posited very near the 5th house or be near the lord of the Lagna, the native will have issues during the prime of youth; otherwise, it will be in his old age.

Q. 90. How do you predict adoption?

Ans. The 9th house must be Ubhaya (common sign) with a strong planet preferably in good amsa, posited in it. The karaka (Sun) must also be in Ucchamsa but unfavourably situated, aspected by a benefic planet. Then the native will be an adopted child.

Q. 91. If the lord of the 5th house is weak and occupies Dusthanas, will the children be weak and ill or will they be useless and a source of misery to parents?

Ans. If the children have to be useless to their parents, the 5th lord should not be weak; on the contrary, he should be powerful but subjected to strong malefic aspects and in dusthanas or bad places.

Q. 92. What are the combinations for stillbirths?

Ans. The following yogas will bring about still-born children: (a) The lord of 9 in a female horoscope fairly strong, while the lord of 5, the house that governs pregnancy, is afflicted by Mars or Ketu; (b) in the Ashtakavarga of Jupiter the fifth house from Jupiter having bindus of planets who are eunuchs in character (Saturn or Mercury); and (c) the fifth house being afflicted by upagrahas like Dhuma or Ketu.

Again, if the house is aspected by the lord of the house wherein Mandi is posited, the result will be still-born children.

Q. 93. How do you predict twins, male twins, female twins and one male and one female?

Ans. When the Moon and Venus are in even signs, and Jupiter, Mars, the ascendant and Mercury happen to be in odd signs, there will be twins, one son and one daughter. When a strong male, planet aspects Lagna or the Moon in even signs, one son and one daughter will be born. If Mars, Mercury, Jupiter occupy even signs and they are powerful, male twins will be born. When all the planets and Lagna occupy rising Navamsa, and Mercury who is posited in Gemini Navamsa aspects the same, three children will be born (2 males and 1 female). When the above-mentioned planets and Lagna posited in rising Navamsa. are aspected by Mercury occupying Virgo Navamsa three children will be born (2 females and 1 male). When all the planets and Lagna occupy Gemini or Sagittarius Navamsa and Mercury posited in Gemini Navamsa aspect the above, three children will be born (3 males). When all the planets and Lagna occupy Virgo or Pisces Navamsa and Mercury posited in Virgo amsa aspects the same, three children will be born (3 females). These are according to Saravali.

Q. 94. How do you find out if a person is a eunuch?

Ans. Eunuchs are of different kinds. Kama Thanthra deals with 20 types. (1) Nisarga Shanda, (2) Badha, (3) Paksha Shanda, (4) Keelaka, (5) Shapadhi Shanda, (6) Sthabdha, (7) Earshaka, (8) Sevyaka, (9) Akshipthabeeja, (10) Moghabeeja, (11) Saleena, (12) Anyapathi, (13) Mukhabhoga, (14) Vatha Rethas, (15) Kumbheeka, (16) Panda, (17) Nashtaka, (18) Asevya, (19) Sugandhi, (20) Shanda.

Persons without linga or the male-sex urge are 'Nisarga' Shanda; persons without anda are Badha; those who are capable of coitus only once a fortnight are called Paksha Shanda; those who enjoy a woman soon after she is enjoyed by another areKeelaka;those who are incapable of coitus because of

Guru-Sapa are called Sapadhi Shanda; those who are incapable of discharging semen are called Sthabdha; those who are capable of coitus only after they observe another doing it are called Earshaka; those who become incapable as the result of extreme sexual indulgences are called Sevyaka; those whose discharge of semen prevents coitus are Akshipthabeeja; those who are incapable of coitus even after women's sexual appeal are Moghabeeja; those who are capable of enjoyment only after he sees sexual intercourse before him are Saleena; those who are capable of enjoying other women are Anyapathi; those who enjoy the facial portion alone are Mukhasa; When 'gas' is generated at the time of coitus, he is called Vatha Rethus; those who enjoy women's hands are Kumbheeka; those who have no erection of the private organ are Panda; those who are incapable of enjoyment because of ill-health are Nashtaka; those whose private organs do not stand erect though capable of discharging semen are Asevya; those who are capable of enjoyment only after smelling the yoni (female sex-organ) of woman or Sushandi; and those who are effeminate in action and form and who have their private organs cut off are called Shandas.

Thus we see in general Kleebhas (eunuchs) are of two types. Some without Beeja and some with Beeja Dosha. When we examine Kleebha Yogas, we have to examine their Beeja Sphuta well.

For details reference may be made to Prasnna Marga.

Q. 95. Suppose a man has many issues. How do you identify the different ones in the horoscope?

Ans. There are many ways. (1) The expired number of amsas of the lord of 5 indicates that number of issues. The order of the number of issues will be the same as the order of Navamsa. Benefic Navamsas indicate surviving children. Benefic Navamsas free from affliction indicate healthy children. Malefic and afflicted Navamsas indicate short-lived children. Exalted Navamsas indicate three children. Swakshetra Navamsas indicate two. The number and order of children can be noted from the planets posited between the 5th house and the house where the lord of the 5th stands. The 5th house is the 1st child. The 3rd house in the same is the 2nd child. The 3rd house in from the 3rd is the 3rd child and so on.

Q. 96. How will you find out from a horoscope of the native will adopt a child?

Ans. Children can be of various types, viz., (1) Aurasa, (2) Kshetraja, (3) Datta, (4) Kreetaka, (5) Krutrima, (6) Adhama, (7) Goodothpanna, (8) Apaviddha, (9) Pounarbhava, (10) Kanina and (11) Sahodba.

(1) Aurasa Putra is a legitimate child born to him through his own wife. (2) When the husband is a eunuch or afflicted by diseases, a child born to his wife through a third person is known as kshetraja. When the 5th house happens to be capricorn or Aquarius or the vargas of Saturn, and Mercury aspects the same without at the same time being the aspect of the Sun, Jupiter or Mars, kshetriya is born. (3) Datta is one taken in accordance with rites of adoption. When the 5th house happens to be Capricorn or Aquarius, Saturn, occupying the same and the Moon aspecting it at the same time, we can say that the native will have adopted child or Datta. (4) Kreetaka is one purchased from other parents in a sale. When the 5th house happens to be Gemini or Virgo and Mercury occupying the same with the Moon aspecting it we have Kreetaka putra. (5) Krutrima putra is one who is taken as one's child through sheer affection. When the 7th house happens to be Aries or Scorpio and the 5th house contains Saturn without the aspect of any other planets, we have Krutrima putra. (6) Adhama putra is one born to a family with a lower status or rank. A child born to a concubine is Adhama putra. When the 5th house happens to be Leo Rasi and the Sun occupies the same aspected by Mars, we have Adhama ulajata (an inability to escape a dificult

situation or one born in a low status). (7) Goodothpahanna is one born to his wife in his own house though the author of his origin is not known. When the Moon occupies Aries or Scorpio and fifth house is aspected by Saturn without the aspect of any other planet Jaraja is born. (8) Apaviddha is one taken by a person when the real parents of the child abandon it. When the 5th house happens to be Capricorn or Aquarius and Mars occupies it and the Sun aspects the same, we have Apaviddha (9) Pounarbhava is one born to a widow or a woman abandoned by the husband. When the moon occupies Capricorn or Aquarius Rasis or Vargas of Saturn and Saturn occupies the 5th house aspected by Venus and the Sun, we have Pounarbhava. (10) Kanina is one born to a woman before the real marriage. When the Moon is very weak and occupies any house and the 5th house is either aspected or conjoined by the Sun, we have Kanina putra. (11) Sahodha is one born to his wife after the necessary rites though the exact origin of the child is not known. When the 5th house happens to be Cancer or Leo or the vargas of the Sun and the Moon and. the Sun or the Moon occupy the same aspected by Venus, we have Sahodha putra. These are some of the types of children and the readers will do well to go through Prasna Marga and Saravali for more particulars.

Q. 97. How do you find out when a debtor will be free from all debts?

Ans. (a) When the lord of 2 and planets posited in the 2 are stronger than the lords of, or planets posited in 6, 8 or 12; or (b) When the evil houses are powerfully aspected by strong benefics, the native will become free from all his debts. This will take place in the Dasas or Bhuktis of planets referred to above causing Rina Bhanga.

Q. 98. How do you delineate the mission for which an individual is born? Also the topic past and future lives may be discussed.

Ans. The answer for the first part of the question depends upon what is considered as one's individual mission. It may be political, religious, social, cultural or something else. Generally, the nature of one's mission in this life can be ascertained by a deep consideration of the 10th house. If planets are powerful there, then the native will succeed in realising the mission. If afflicted there will be many hitches.

Regarding past and future lives, books like Brihat Jataka gives some interesting information. The causes of death are also enumerated. If at a person's birth the 12th house or its lord be in a house or Navamsa owned by a benefic or be associated with a benefic, death will be a happy one free from sufferings. If the Sun and the Moon are the lords of the 12th-house or occupy the 12th house the future world indicated is Kailasa. If the planet in question be Venus, it is Swarga or heaven. If Mars be the planet it is the earth; Mercury-Vaikunta; Saturn-Yama's world; Jupiter-Brahma Loka. Rahu and Ketu- Hell. If the lord of the 9th or 5th house occupy exaltation or own house or Lagna, then it should be stated that the native's previous and future birth (according as it is the 9th or 5th house considered) must be that of a human being. If the two planets namely lord of the 9th and 5th are in association, the native should have his birth in his own place. There are several other particulars governing the question of death and the past or future lives.

Q. 99. Rahu and Ketu are supposed to own no signs but Rahu has been given Virgo. What is your authority on the subject?

Ans. Parasara gives the sign 'Virgo' to Rahu. Most of the ancient authors, of **Saravali, Jataka Parijatha, Jyotishthathwa, Bhavakuthuhala** etc., agree in assigning Virgo to Rahu though they differ in Uchcha Rasis. Ketu is the lord of Pisces Rasi.

Q. 100. Which houses and planets are to be considered when discussing previous and after births?

Ans. Mantreswara is of opinion that the sign wherein the lord of 9 is posited marks the previous state of existence. The Rasi wherein the lord of 5 is posited marks the future state of existence.

Some take the 12th house as the previous birth, and 2nd as the next birth. By examining both these, life regarding previous or next birth can be read. Parasara gives importance to the Navamsa chart, and the Navamsa of the Moon as indicating previous birth.

Q. 101. Is there any truth in the belief that after a person passes his 32nd year, Janma Rasi should be taken as Lagna in reading a horoscope?

Ans. This is the view taken by Varahamihira. Till the 32nd year, Lagna and what is implied by it prevails. The person will be more conc rned, with his physical body. After his 32nd year, his mind becomes fully ripe and all bis actions are regulated by the mind. After the 64th year, he becomes conscious of something higher, viz., Atman, and all his actions are controlled by it. Hence from the 64th year, Surya Lagna is more important than the other two.

Q. 102. Are the general results produced by Rahu in Capricorn more favourable than if he were in Aquarius though the latter is its Moolathrikona according to some?

Ans. Aquarius cannot be considered the Moolathrikona of Rahu, although many people do it. Even these authors when describing the Dasa effects do not seem to give good effects for Aquarius. As for authority that Rahu produces good results in Capricorn, there is the time-honored tradition in Kerala that Makara (Capricorn) Rahu is the "Royal Rahu".

Q. 103. What planetary influences assist us to aspire for the following: New acquaintances, letters from friends and relatives, meeting with friends and relatives,

unnecessary exchange of words, non-availability of cooked food or beds for sleeping.

Ans. New acquaintances-Friends of the lord of Lagna and their connection with 11 house-Mercury.

Letters from friends: Connection of 2nd house with the 11th House-Mercury.

Meeting with friends and relatives: Mercury, Lagna and Lagna Navamsa.

Unnecessary exchange of words-The lord of 2, 2nd house and Mercury in inimical houses or in the house of weak Mars.

Non-availability of cooked food or beds: 3rd house governs meals. Any affliction of these will bring in non-availability of food. The Moon also has to be included. The 12th house and Venus determine comfort for sleep. Affliction to these results in uncomfortable or no beds.

CHAPTER - III

Marriage

Q. 104. What are the possible indications for marriage? What factors do you take into account for predicting the date?

Ans. The 7th house and the lord of 7 must be strong, well-placed and free from affliction. Venus is the Karaka for the wife and Saturn to a certain extent is the Karaka for the husband. They also must be well-posited. In Venus Ashtakavarga the 7th house should be free from the bindus or marks of eunuchs. Presence of more than 5 bindus is highly favoured. The 7th house from the Moon and Venus should also be noted in this way. Note when Venus and the lords of 7 from Lagna, the Moon and Venus transit the above mentioned Rasis. Their Dasas and Bhuktis also may be noted.

Q. 105. How do you predict marriage with (a) a well-behaved girl and (b) a wicked girl?

Ans. As a general rule, the. following holds good. If 7th bhava from Lagna be either in Mars' house or Amsa and if the planet owning the Amsa of 7th bhava be either weak or eclipsed, the wife will become vicious in her youth. But if the same be located in the Rasi or Amsa of a benefic planet, the wife will be virtuous. If aspected by benefic planets also, all the better for her character.

Q. 106. How do you find out the month and year of marriage from horoscopes?

Ans. The whole horoscope should be examined with reference to chances of marriage, whether early, ordinary, or late marriage and Dasa bhuktis worked out and transits also considered. Here are a few rules which may be useful. Add together the figures for the lords of the Lagna and 7th bhava. Find the Rasi and Navamsa indicated by the result. When Jupiter transit the Rasi so found, an astrologer may predict a person's marriage. The time of marriage may also be determined in the same way from the total of the figures for the lords of the Rasi occupied by the Moon and the 7th bha va. Of the two planets that are the lords respectively of the Rasi and Navamsa occupied by the lord of the 7th Bhava, find which is stronger. During the Dasa period of that planet, the marriage of the person may take place when Jupiter traverses Trikona of the Rasi and Amsa occupied by the lord of the 7th bhava. Again find the stronger of the two planets, Venus and the Moon. During the Dasa period of the stronger planet the period favourable for marriage may be found in a similar manner.

"If the lord of the 7th bhava be associated with Venus, its Dasa and Bhukti may lead to marriage. Failing that, Dasa and Bhukti of the lord of the Rasi occupied by the planet owning the 2nd bhava may effect the marriage. The Dasa and Bhukti of the lords of the 10th and 9th bhavas come next in order. Lastly note the planet associated with the lord of the 7th bhava or the one occupying it. During the Dasa and Bhukti of one of these, marriage may take place." 'If the planet powerful for producing marriage be benefic and in a benefic house, it will bring on the happy event at the commencement of its Dasa. If the planet being benefic should occupy a malefic house, the marriage will take place in the middle of the Dasa. If the planet and the house it occupies are both malefic, the event in question will happen at the end of its Dasa. But if the planet in question occupies a benefic house and be in conjunction with a benefic planet at the same time, its influence for good will prevail during the whole of its Dasa period.

Another indication for the time of marriage is obtained thus-Find out the order of sign representing the 7th bhava from Aries and add 8 to this. The resulting figure added to multiples of 5 will generally be the age of marriage.

Q. 107. How do you predict if and when divorce may take place?

Ans. There are combinations which provide for the wife being rejected by husband as unfaithful or for other reasons or for the wife abandoning her husband. The wife is likely to be abandoned by her husband if the 7th bhava from Lagna in case of male or first bhava in the case of woman be either in Mars' house or amsa. Or if the plane owning the Amsa of the 7th bhava be either wealth or eclipsed, the woman concerned may become vicious in her youth and may be rejected by her husband.

Q. 108. Can you say from a particular horoscope if the native will marry a particular girl?

Ans. Yes. There are many ways of ascertaining this. Jatakadesa gives the following:

(a) Add up the longitudes of the lord of 1 and Venus. From this find out the constellation and this will be the Nakshatra of the wife.

OR

(b) Add up the longitudes of the lords of I and VII and find out the Nakshatra. This will be the constellation of the wife.

(c) Calculate the strongest of the following:

(i) The Rasi, wherein the lord of 7 is posited, (ii) Its Navamsa Rasi, (iii). Its house of exaltation, (iv) Its house of deblitation, (v) Rasi wherein Venus is posited, (vi) The 7th Rasi from 5, (vii) The Dwadasama Rasi of the Moon, (viii) The Trikona Rasis, and (ix) The Rasi wherein you find more bindus in Chandrashtakavarga. Find the Samudayashtaka Varga of these ten factors. The strongest Rasi will be the Lagna of the wife.

(d) The Rasi 'Dik' of the wife is to be determined from the Rasi wherein the lord of 7 stands or from the planet that stands in or aspects 7.

Q. 109. How do you predict marriage with?

(a) virgin widows;

(b) widows with encumbrance.

Ans. (a) If in the male horoscope, the 7th house from Venus has a planet aspected by a powerful Mars, we can say he will marry a virgin widow. He should also have his 7th house strong and. free from affliction.

(b) If in the male horoscope, the 5th house from Venus aspected by Mars is strong and free from affliction, we can say that the widow has given birth to children that are living.

Q. 110. How do you predict unnatural desire for sexual enjoyment such as homosexuality, lesbianism, sodomy etc?

Ans. If Venus happens to be the lord of the Rasi where in Gulika is posited and occupies strong positions as 10 or 4, he will have desire for unnatural enjoyment. When Saturn and Gulika occupy the 7th, the same result.

Q. 111. From which house or planet do you predict a second marriage?

Ans. Venus and the 7th house indicate first marriage. If you are sure that the first will either die or separate from the hu band, take the planets in 7 or associated with Venus. The strongest will determine the 2nd wife. In a female horoscope, take Saturn in the place of Venus (Prasna Marga). Some authors want us to read the 11th house and this also may be adopted.

Q. 112. Which bhavas and planets indicate wives?

Ans. The 7th house and Venus indicate 'wives'. The Sun also governs 'marriages' according to Prasna Marga. The number is to be determined from the strength of the Bhavas and planets. Nature of the wives is to be looked through 'vargas'. The following lines are culled out from Prasna Marga. There will be re-marriage when (a) two planets occupy 11 and Mercury and Saturn occupy 7; (b) Lagna is a common sign or when the lord of 7 and the Moon occupy a common sign or Navamsa; (c) Sun and Mars occupy 7 or have their Navamsa in 7; this will result in the death or separation of first wife and a second marriage; (d) The lords of 7 either from Lagna or Moon and Venus are favourably and strongly posited, there will be three marriages; (e) If the lord of 7 or Venus is in exaltation and two or more planets occupy 7, there will. be three or more marriages.

Q. 113. It is said that lords of 1 and 9 in association will produce benefic results and more so, when aspected by the lord of the 10th. Should these lords be in the same degree and the lord of the 10th exactly in the 180th degree from the lords of 1 and 9?

Ans. According to Hindu Astrology, conjunction implies the presence of two planets in a sign. The conjunction-rather association of lords of 1 and 9, will produce a Raja Yoga. By aspect is meant, the aspect on the sign in which the association occurs. When a planet is in the 7th sign from another, an aspect is formed. If the aspecting angle is 180°, then a powerful aspect is formed. In association, if the distance between the conjoined bodies is wide, say about 25 degrees, the effects of the yoga will be feeble. The nearer they are, the more pronounced will be the results. In judging the intensity of yogas, the special aspects of Jupiter, Mars and Saturn should also be considered.

Q. 114. (a) If the lords of 8 or 9 from Lagna and the Moon join a sign, does it produce good results?

(b) What are the effects of Konadhipathi and Kendradhipathi in Dusthanas?

Ans. (a) The lord of 8, wherever he stands, or whatever he aspects, destroys the effect of the house be occupies or the planet he aspects.

If the lord of 8 is strong, the good effects of the planet as such (without reference to the houses where it is posited or aspects) will come to pass in its Dasa or Bhukthi periods. If the lord of 8 is weak, none of the good effects will be felt. Only bad results will be felt.

If the lord of 11 is strong, good effects alone will be experienced. If it is weak; good effects will be least felt. If the lord of 8 is strong and occupies a Dusthana, evil effects will be greater. In this way, read the effects of the lord of 3, 6, 8 and 12.

(b) The lords of 9 and 5 in Dusthanas will be bad whether the planets be evil or good by nature. The lords of Kendras also will give the same results as above. Here Dusthana means 6, 8 and 12. The lord of 1 in Dusthana will bring only evil.

Q. 115. Does a planet lose its strength if hemmed in between malefics?

The planet does not lose its strength but its power for evil strength (Papa Bala) increases.

In all such cases readers should be careful to differentiate between ownership and occupation. There are two types of malefics-malefics by nature and malfics by ownership. The lordships of 3 and 11 do not come under Dusthanadhipathya.

Q. 116. Which house governs education, the 4th or the 5th?

Ans. According to Prasna Marga and all the commentaries of Parasara Hora the 4th house is said to govern "education". The 5th house indicates 'intelligence' or medha; If this can be included in education, then the 5th house can also be said to indicate "Vidya".

Q. 117. The sutra: Atmadhikaha Kaladibhirnabhogaha sapthanamashtanamva is explained as meaning that the planet which gets the highest number of degrees will be Atmakaraka. The commentator for explaining this sutra has relied on Vriddha and Parasara which I think he ought not to have done when the original sutra is clear. What is the real meaning of the sutra? Should we take merely the degrees or minutes and seconds while deciding the Karaka?

Ans. A sutra is defined by Prof. B. Suryanarain Rao as "the shortest in form with the largest meaning possible". The brevity of a Sutra is its distinguishing feature and in order to understand its true meaning the aid of authoritative commentators is absolutely necessary. The above Sutra simply means that of the seven (or eight including Rahu) planets, whichever gets the highest degrees (of course in a sign) becomes the atmakaraka. The author has used the word KALA which clearly means degree. When the planets are in the same degree, take the minutes, when the minutes are also the same, take seconds. If two or more planets obtain the same Karakatwa by virtue of being situated in the same degree, minute and second, then, vacancies caused by such contingencies are filled up by Rahu in the reverse order or the natural karakas as defined by Parasara. Suppose in a horoscope two planets have the same (highest) number of degrees, minutes and seconds. Then both of them become merged together into one, viz., Atmakaraka. Then a vacancy will be caused. This will be supplied by Rahu. If there is a further vacancy, fill it up by the Naisargika or natural karaka. For more details, see STUDIES IN JAIMINI ASTROLOGY by Dr. B. V. Raman.

Q. 118. When Jupiter gets maraka-dosha (death inflicting power) by being lord of Kendra (angle) and if

he occupies trines or angles, will not the evil influences disappear?

Ans. Jupiter should not be considered a maraka imply because he owns kendras. He becomes evil by such quadrangular ownership but this does not qualify him to inflict death unless he is otherwise empowered to do so by location or ownership from chandra Lagna- As a natural benefic he does good but as owning Kendra he will also give rise to evil results, particularly with reference to the indications of the 4th and 7th houses.

Q. 119. Planets are said to be weak when they are placed in the last Navamsa of a Rasi. If Venus occupies Pisces or Meena in both Rasi and Navamsa, does he not become weak because he will be in the last Navamsa?

Ans. Residence in the last part of a sign no doubt goes under the name of Peedya and such a disposition is not productive of good. But each rule has an exception. In the instance quoted even though Venus is in the last part of a sign, there are two good circumstances which counteract the Peedya Avasta, viz. (1) Venus gets exalted in Navamsa and (2) the position goes under the technical name of Vargottama, a very suspicious disposition. Hence the ordinary definition for the Peedya state does not apply in this case.

Q. 120. (a) In books comming from Raman Publications more prominence is given to trines than kendras. But in practical dealing of horoscopes in The Astrological Magazine, kendras are prominently dealt with. Why?

(b) What is meant by planets below the horizon;

(c) What are the effects of Gulika?

Ans. (a) Kendras and trines are both important. If all the kendras are occupied by planets, the horoscope receives considerable strength and such a disposition goes under the special distinction of Chatussagara Yoga indicating a smooth career in life. Kendras play a significant part. Some of the malefic yogas such as Kemadruma are capable of being counteracted by the mere presence of a planet in a kendra. Benefic in kendras can act as a powerful antidote for even Balarishta. It is on account of this that kendras are given an important place. Moreover several yogas are caused by the dispositions of planets in mutual kendras. Some astrologers say that Trikona becomes important when taken along with a kendra. But this view has not won acceptance. Location of a planet in a trikona is no doubt good but union of the lordship of a kendra and trikona gets special dignity. In actual practice trikona is as important as kendra because in the formation of certain yogas, a planet should occupy either a kendra or a trikona. For example if the lord of the Lagna, the Sun and the Moon, being in a kendra or a trikona occupy an exaltation, own or friendly house, the resulting yoga is Srikanta. Thus kendras and konas are both important in their own way.

(b) Planets situated between the 1st and the 7th house counted in the anticlockwise direction are supposed to be below the horizon. As everyone knows, the second house rises or ascends after the Lagna. In other words, the second and subsequent houses are below the horizon when the ascendant is rising and the descendant or the 7th house is setting. Thus all the signs between the ascendant and descendant (in the anticlockwise direction), viz., 12th, 11th, 10th, 9th, 8th and 7th are above the horizon while the rest are below the horizon.

(c) Ancient writers have not attached much significance to Gulika. Reference to this is to be found mostly in Tamil books on astrology. Mandi or Gulika plays an important part in the determination of Lagna (in doubtful cases), maraka planets and also in finding out the probable period of death. Gulika in different Bhavas gives the following results: 1st Bhava-cruel, thief, devoid of modesty, voracious eater, deformed eye, irritable nature; 2nd-quarrelsome, will be poor, not true to his word and devoid of wealth; 3rd-ill-tempered, unsocial, ostentatious, devoid of brothers and sisters; 4th unfortunate and poor; 5th-fickle minded, badly disposed; 6th-brave, versed in Kshudra Mantras and a terror to his foes; 7th-quarrelsome, loose morals, ungrateful; 8th-weak and impaired eyes; 9th-unhappy on account of children and deserted by them; 10th-heterodoxical tendencies having no faith in religion, miserly; 11th-happiness, children, power and plenty; 12th-poor, will have high expenditure, dislikes sexual pleasures.

The above is culled out from an ancient astrological work.

Q. 121. How do you reconcile the position of a kendra planet if the planet lies in a kendra in Rasi Chakra and Kona (trines) in Bhava Chakra?

Ans. Asraya effects are to be told for Rasi Chakra and Bhava effects for Bhava Chakra. The two should not be mixed. Yogas wherein Rasi effects are to be looked into, must be only those caused by the position of planets in Rasis. Yogas caused by Bhava positions are quite different from those brought about by Rasi positions. Ancient authors have clearly pointed out these when describing yogas. Where no explicit mention is made, the reference is to the Bhava positions only.

Q. 122. Can a Bhavadhipati (house-lord) get strength if he is in a kendra or trikona or upachaya from his own house?

Ans. It is stated in Jatakadesa that the Bhava effects will exist only if the lords of the various Bhavas occupy a kendra (angle) or trikona (trine) or upachaya from the respective Bhavas and the existing effects will be experienced by the native if they occupy a kendra, trikona or upachaya from Lagna. If a Bhavadhipati (house lord) occupies the twelfth, second or eighth from the Bhava concerned, the effects will not materialise. Even if they occupy kendras, trikonas or upachayas from Lagna, very little good will be experienced.

Suppose a man is born in Mithuna (Gemini) Lagna and Venus and Mercury are in Aries, Mars is in Capricorn. Here Mercury is the lord of 1 and 4. Mars is the lord of 6 and 11. The lord of 4 is in the 8th house from the Bhava (house) and 11th house from Lagna. The lord of 11 is in the 10th house from the Bhava and the 8th house from Lagna. Because the lord of 4 is in the 8th house from the Bhava, the Bhava effects of 4 will not exist. If at all, it will exist only nominally. And the little may be experienced by the native as he is in the 11th house from Lagna. In the 2nd case, the lord of 11 occupies the 10th house from the Bhava. As such all the 11th house effects will potentially exist in the horoscope. There will be good income and many elder brothers, but none of these may be actually enjoyed by the native, as the lord of 11 is in the 8th from Lagna. We shall take one more example. Suppose Jupiter occupies Aquarius and the Ascendant is Cancer. The lord of 9 is in the 12th from the Bhava (house) and the 8th from Lagna. Consequently, 9th house effects will not exist in the horoscope and the native may not experience any of the 9th house effects.

Q. 123. Saturn in the 11th house is said to be good for wealth and longevity. Is it also good for health?

Ans. Saturn in 11 is good for wealth and longevity. But it is bad for health according to Parasara Hora.

Q. 124 In Bhavartha Chandrika, it is said that Saturn in 2 makes one a fool and a villain. According to Bhargava Samhita Saturn in 2 makes one learned. How do you reconcile these two statements?

Ans. Ancient authors generally emphasize different aspects of the question in their own way. According to Bhavartha Chandrika, Saturn, if weak and afflicted, makes one a fool and a villain. If he is strong and well aspected, he makes one learned. Saturn a malefic by nature can become a benefic by position and strength. In such seemingly contradictory statements, we have to be guided by the explanation given by other authors. In Skanda Hora for instance, it has been specially stated that a strong Saturn is not evil but capable of doing good. Saturn gives good Raja Yogas in certain positions.

Q. 125. The 2ⁿᵈ and the 7ᵗʰ houses in a horoscope are maraka houses. At the same time they represent wealth and martial happiness. In view of these apparently conflicting characteristics of the houses, what results would the lords of 2 and 7 give during their periods?

Ans. Maraka houses do not always cause death. Only when the lords of 8 from Lagna and the Moon are incapable of bestowing death, do we have to look to maraka houses. Sometimes planets in 12 cause death. When these do not cause death, maraka houses and planets posited in the same bring about death.

When marakas are divested of maraka functions, predict by their nature, the nature of wealth and marital happiness. Remember Venus is the karaka for marital happiness and Jupiter is the karaka of wealth. These also should be carefully examined.

Some authors are of the opinion that both death and wealth can be told at the time of maraka Dasas. For example, a man may earn much and may win a lottery prize or even become a king and all of a sudden he may also pass away. Though such cases are few, they do happen. In such cases marakas will have apamrityu doshas.

Q. 126. The lord of 11ᵗʰ is said to produce unhappy results. Since the 11ᵗʰ is the house of gains shauld not the 11ᵗʰ lord produce good results?

Ans. "The lord of 11 whether he is a benefic or malefic will produce evil results." So says Parasara. "He is not as bad as the lords of 6, 8 or 3, or the benefic lords of 4 and 7." The only explanation that can be found for this apparent contradiction is: if the lord, of 11 is a benefic and posited in good and favourable houses, he will bring in gains. There can be no gain without evil. The mere wish for gain is evil.

Q. 127. When a benefic planet owning bad houses is exalted in a benefic house (favourable) or a benefic owning good houses is exalted in an unfavourable house or a malefic ruling good houses is exalted in a bad house, what will be the effect of the planet with reference to the houses it owns, the house where it is posited, and the house which it aspects. Should a planet owning a bad house be weak if it should give benefic results with reference to the said houses?

Ans. These points have been raised and answered by the author of Prasna Marga in Chapter XIV. According to him the following general rules have to be carefully noted: A benefic (a subha by nature). Wherever he may be will improve the house he occupies. But in so doing bis qualities and karaka nature will get weakened by his contact with bad houses (unfavourable houses for a subha are 3, 6, 8 and 12). Thus planets occupying these houses will give out evil in their Dasa periods.

A malefic (papa by nature)-Wherever he maybe, he will destroy the house he occupies. But in so doing, his qualities will get improved by his contact with good houses. (Favourable houses for a malefic are 3, 6 and 11. When dealing with diseases, 6 also is unfavourable). Thus evil planets occupying these houses will give out good in their Dasa periods.

With regard to ownership, 6, 8 and 12 alone are bad. The lords of these, wherever they may be, will destroy the Bhavas they occupy or aspect. Here 'lords' mean both subhas and papas.

Parasara and his followers attribute evil to benefics if they own Kendras, while malefics are good if they own Kendras. Trikonas are good for both. 3, 6, 8 are bad for all. The lordship of 12 is indifferent by itself. Here it should be clearly borne in.mind, that the good or evil arising from the lordships above mentioned is not permanent but only temporary. It will show itself in the Dasa periods of the various lords.

With regard to the strength it should be clearly understood that the stronger the planet (whether good or bad) the more good it will do. Whether the native will experience these effects is to be determined from the position of planets from Lagna or Chandra (the stronger of the two).

With this background, questions can be answered easily. For a man born in Libra with Jupiter in Cancer the effects will be (1) Jupiter strengthens the 10th house and all the houses which it aspects;(2) the houses which it owns; viz., 3 and 6 are also strengthened; (3) all the good qualities of the planet will be experienced by the native; (4) in Jupiter Dasa calculated according to Nakshatra Paksha the evil effects resulting from the ownership of 3 and 6 will be felt by the man. This will be temporary and never throughout life.Similarly for Venus in Pisces for Sagittarius and Pisces Lagnas. For a man born in Sagittarius with Jupiter in Cancer, the effects will be: Jupiter improves the 8th house. Thereby his life is lengthened. Being a subha, the houses which he aspects are also improved. As he occupies an unfavourable house, all his karaka qualities will not be visible in the life of the native. His Dasa periods will be evil because of his ownership of 1 and 4 and his occupation of 8. Still Jupiter will give potentially everything connected with the houses he rules and aspects, though none of those potential effects for good will be enjoyed by the native (here it should be noted that the potential effects for evil will be least as the lord is strong and exalted).

For a person born in Taurus Lagna with Saturn in Libra-as the planet is in the 6th house it is spoiled (diseases, enemies and debts increase) but as the planet is strong, the evil effects of 6 will be considerably minimised. As the planet is in 6 all the qualities inherent in Saturn will be visible since it is a favourable house for him and the native will experience all the effects of Saturn in his life (Saturn governs iron, goods, servants, etc.)

The house he aspects will be spoiled a little though the bad effects will be least as he is exalted. The Dasa periods also will be brilliant.

N.B. We should note that when considering diseases, 6 is not a favourable house for malefics. Hence sickness and diseases in that part of the body indicated by 6 should also be anticipated.

For a person born in Taurus Lagna with Jupiter in Cancer, Jupiter both improves and spoils the 3rd house. As a subha he improves and as the lord of 8 he destroys the house he occupies and aspects. As he is in an unfavourable house from Lagna, none of the karaka significations will be enjoyed by the native. As he is exalted all those things that he governs, viz., (1) as the lord of 8 and 11 and (2) being posited in 3 and aspecting 9, 7 and 11 will reside potentially in the horoscope in full. If he is weak, the above-mentioned things will be less. In the Dasa periods, he is almost evil. If weak, his evil nature will be doubled in the Dasa periods.

Q. 128. What are the Bhava Phalas of Mercury in the 12th house in general? Do you agree with the results mentioned in Chamathkara Chinthamani by Narayana Bhatta?

Ans. Though Varahamihira may not accept the views of Narayana Bhatta completely, there is no contradiction. Mihira in his Bhavamadhya states that when Mercury occupies the 12th house, he will give the results of the Sun when the latter is in 12, i.e., Pathitha. Narayana Bhatta mentions that one will overcome one's enemies, besides improving wealth in different ways, and that one will also associate oneself with learned and godly men. A Pathitha (an outcaste) can have all these. South Indian astrologers say that Mercury in 12 make one a learned man. Parasara too does not say anything against this. In Chamathkara Chinthamani, the author emphasizes more the aspect of planets than their position.

Q. 129. In Hindu Predictive Astrology, only seven planets are considered for Ashtakavarga. "Ashta" means eight but not seven. The total bind us (dots) are taken to be 337 relating to seven planets. Which is the other planet to make eight? Is it Lagna or Rahu?

Ans. Ashtakavarga deals with only 7 planets. Favourable places from each of the seven planets and Lagna make up 337. 'Ashta' refers to 'places' and not planets. Rahu is mentioned to have 43 bindus or favourable positions according to Jatakasyamasangraha. There is no mention of Rahu either in Brihat Jataka or Parasara Hora. In calculating 43 for Rahu Aahtakavarga, favourable places from Rahu are not taken into consideration. Rahu Ashtakavarga is as follows:

Favourable places from:

Sun	....	1-2-3-5-7-8-10	(7)
Moon	....	1-3-5-7-8-9-10	(7)
Mars	....	1-3-5-12	(4)
Mercury	....	2-4-7-8-12	(5)
Jupiter	....	1-3-4-6-8	(5)
Venus	....	6-7-11-12	(4)
Saturn	....	3-5-7-10-11-12	(6)
Ascendant	....	3-4-5-9-12	(5)

Q. 130. How can you find out if the house (residence) you occupy is subject to evil (malefic) influences?

Find out the Rasi of the house from the name that you have given to the house. If this Rasi is movable, Jupiter stands in the 9th house; if it is fixed, Jupiter is in the Rasi itself; if it is common, then Jupiter is in the 5th house. Keep these spots in the house or compound neat and clean. Consider that the Graha Devata dwells in the spots mentioned above. If these spots are kept unclean knowingly or otherwise, evil will befall the persons who dwell in the house.

Nakshatra or constellation of the house that you occupy can also be found out by the name given to the house. From the constellation, we can fix the position of the Moon. When Saturn passes through Anishta Rasis in transit, evil will happen as death or sale of vehicles, animals, etc.When Jupiter passes through Anishta Rasis, predict evil to children or the finance of the occupant.

When Rahu passes through unfavourable houses, danger from reptiles can be expected. When Mars passes through the same, danger from fire is indicated.

When three or more evil planets pass through Anishta Rasis, madness to the members of the house can be stated. When Gulika passes through Anishta Rasis, evil spirits cause trouble.

Q. 131. How do you read births other than of human beings?

Ans. We can safely ascert that the birth is of a viyoni (asexual) type if all the following conditions are seen :

(1) All natural malefics must be powerful and all natural benefics must be weak.

(2) Moon must be weak.

(3) Mercury and Saturn must occupy Kendras or aspect Lagna.

(4) Either Lagna or Janma Rasi must be a Viyoni Rasi.

Having assured yourself that the birth is not of human beings, examine the Dwadasamsa of the Moon and the birth will be appropriate to the Dwadasamsa Rasi. If it is Aries, it is sheep, if it is Taurus; it is oxen; if it is Pisces 'fish' and so on. Regarding birds, if Lagna Rasi is in Pakshi Drekkana, you can say that the birth is that of a bird. Similarly you can understand the nature and growth of trees. If Lagna, Sun, Moon and

Jupiter are weak while others are strong, you can say the birth is of 'trees'. The nature of the trees will depend on the planets and the Rasis wherein they stand.

Some authors take the Navamsa of Lagna or the Moon to determine the nature of births. (Note that births are of four kinds: (1) Udbhija (trees, planets etc.), (2) Jarayuja (men and beasts), (3) Swedaja (vermin type) and (4) Andaja (birds). All these can be read from the Dwadasamsa or Navamsa of Lagna and Moon. For more details, the readers may refer to Saravali.

Q. 132. How is the birth Lagna found from the lines on the palm? How are the planetary positions obtained from the reading of the palm?

Ans. To find birth Lagnas from the palm, lines on the phalanges are counted and then divided by 12 and the remainder shows the zodiacal sign rising at birth. Also for finding out the positions of planets from the palm many such calculations are to be made, which cannot be fully explained in short answers. You may study Astro Palmistry by Mihiracharya which will fully explain these points.

Q. 133. Which hand should be examined in the case of women, the right or the left?

Ans. In all cases, whether for male or female, both hands are to be considered to come to a correct conclusion.

Q. 134. Where do we find the lines in the palm marked for brothers, sisters, father and mother and how do we find out if they are living or dead?

Ans. In Hindu Palmistry the father is indicated by the modern "Life-line" and the mother by the "Head-line". The life and fortune are shown according to the development and course of these lines. The short lines on the Mount of Mars on the percussion side of the hand will indicate by the straight and slanting lines, brothers and sisters respectively. When these are cut or crossed we can make out if they are dead. But to find out if they are alive or dead at any specified time, calculations of horoscopes from the lines on the hand will help.

PART - II

PART - II

CHAPTER - I

Vocation

Q. 1. How are predictions on profession made? There are differences of opinion on this point.

Ans. Some read profession from the 10th house from the Ascendant or the Moon. Some read it from the Navamsa lord of the lord of the 10th. The first house also indicates profession in 'Prasna'. All these have to be looked into and the strongest one indicates 'profession'.

Q. 2. From which Bhava or planet can the place or direction of one's livelihood be ascertained?

Ans. Ordinarily the 10th Bhava is the one that denotes all particulars relating to one's livelihood including the place or direction; the sign that is found on the cusp of that Bhava determines the place or direction one has to look to for the line of least resistance.As regards. the planets, the matter is somewhat more complicated. The lord of the 10th Bhava is in some Navamsa. The lord of that Amsa is one of the planets that have major significance. The sign in which that lord is placed, the lord of the 10th, and also the sign in which the Sun is located have also subsidiary importance. All these influences have to be carefully blended and judged in the case of a particular horoscope and the dominant direction is to be taken note of before prediction as regards place or direction of profession can be made. If the Moon is strong, the above has to be applied from the position of the Moon also.

Q. 3. What makes one an actor or a singer?

Ans: Generally Venus will have to be strong in the horoscope before one can be a good actor or singer. If this is to be adopted as profession, Venus must be intimately connected with the 10th Bhava in some way or other, e.g., if Venus occupies the 4th or 10th Bhava or if Venus aspects the 10th house, or if Venus is conjoined with the lord of the 10th, his means of livelihood will be singing or acting.

Q. 4. What would make one a leather merchant and an iron merchant?

Ans. When the 10th house is a Jeeva Rasi, we have leather. When the 10th is owned and occupied by Jupiter, we have leather. The Sun and Saturn deal with iron. Mars too is the same.

Jeeva Rasis are Gemini, Virgo, Sagittarius and Pisces.

Dhatu Rasis are Aries, Cancer', Libra and Capricorn.

When these Rasis happen to be the 10th, we will have leather for the first group and iron for the second group. KRISHNEEYA and PRASNA MARGA give more details. There are different opinions regarding planets. Rahu we can include as a Dhatu Graha. Mercury and Jupiter are Jeeva Grahas. Find out the Jeeva Rasi and its connection with Mercury and Jupiter. You have a leather merchant. Find out Dhatu Rasi and its connection with the Moon, Mars, Saturn and Rahu. We have iron goods.

Q. 5. How can you say from a particular horoscope that a man will prosper in mining business?

Ans. All movable signs indicate Dhatus. The Moon, Mars, Saturn and Rahu are Dhatu Grahas. Aswini, Rohini, Punarvasu, Makha, Hasta, Visakha, Moola, Sravana and Poorvabhadra are Dhatu Nakshatras. When the house of wealth or house of property is a movable sign, and when Dhatu Grahas are posited in the same and when the sphuta of 2 or 4 indicate Dhatu constellations, you can say that the native is an owner of mines.

When the 10th house has Dhatu connections as above and then say that the native is employed in mines. The Vargas of the 2nd, 4th and 10th houses may be examined-PRASNA MARGA.

Q. 6. How to read from a horoscope that a person is prospering in (a) magic-mesmerism,(b) hotel-keeping, (c) toddy-selling?

Ans. (a) Rahu governs magic and mesmerism. If he occupies the 10th house or aspects it, we can say that is earnings are through magic or mesmerism. (b) Mars governs hotels. If the native's horoscope has more of Martian Vargas in the 10th house, predict that he is a hotel keeper. Aries governs the same. (c) Toddy Selling: Aquarius governs toddy. Scorpio also governs liquor. Amongst the planets Saturn and Rahu determine toddy.

Q. 7. How to predict from the birth-chart gain or loss in (a) lotteries, (b) speculation,(c) gambling, (d) bargain of lands and buildings,(e) insurance and (f) dowries?

Ans. (a) Lotteries: The 4th and 9th houses represent lotteries. Libra also governs the same. Amongst the planets, Venus and Jupiter may be said to represent the same. The lords of the 4th and 9th and planets posited in the 4th and 9th can also be looked into. We should bear in mind that these should be strong and occupy favourable places, especially the 11th. If there is Parivarthana Yoga of these lords, there are prospects of getting lotteries or hidden treasures. (b) Speculation: The 5th house represents speculation. The 7th house also can be included. Here again, Venus plays a prominent part. (c) Gambling: Gemini, Libra and Aquarius represent gambling and gambling houses. Mercury, Venus and Saturn-all these stand for different types of gambling. The 8th and 12th houses govern the same. (d) Bargain of lands and building: The 4th house represents these; Mars governs lands and. Venus stands for building. (e) Insurance: Saturn and the 8th house stand for insurance. (f) Dowries: The 8th house or 2nd house from Venus stands for dowries.

In all these, we should bear in mind that Rasis, Bhavas and the lords of the above should be strong, well posited both from Lagna and the Bhavas referred to. It is safer that these are connected with the 11th in some way.

Q. 8. Explain how to determine whether one will take to smithy or carpentry as a means of livelihood.

Ans. Saturn governs iron, the Sun governs wood, Mercury, workmanship in arts. The 10th House or Vargas should have the connection of Saturn and Mercury for smithy and the Sun and Mercury for carpentry.

Q. 9. How to predict transfers in a horoscope?

Ans. The question of transfer includes a transfer from one place to another, from one job to another, change to higher or lower grades, and shifting from one house to another. For all these, the Lagna has to be examined; we should see whether it is movable or fixed. Whether it is Urdhwamukha, Sirshodaya or Prushtodaya; whether any movable planet transits it at the time; whether it is afflicted or strengthened. A study of the lord of the ascendant must also be made.

If it is a professional transfer, the 10th lord and the planet is the 10th, both from the Ascendant and the Moon must be carefully looked into. If it is a change of residence from one, house to another, the 4th house lord may be examined. If it is a change from one place to another study the 3rd and 9th houses and their lords. If it is a question of voluntary exile and return, study the 7th, 8th, 9th and their lords. If it is banishment or forcible exile, study the 12th house and its lord. In all these, the Lagna (Ascendant) must also be analysed. When you study these, take care to see the Gochara position of the native and influence of Dasa and Antardasanathas, at the time. Place before you 'Prasthara Ashtakavarga' and fix up the time.

Q. 10. What planets and Rasis govern ships and shipbuilding and how to predict the ownership of ships?

Ans. Cancer and Pisces are watery signs and watery Drekkanas may be taken to indicate ships and shipbuilding. Amongst the planets, Venus and the Moon govern these. In PRASNA MARGA, Drekkanas are given more prominence.

Q. 11. How to judge success or failure in a lottery?

Ans. The lord of the 4th should be in the Vargas of the lord of the 11th. He should be strong and posited in the 11th house or 5th house.

Q. 12. What makes one an engineer, agricultural demonstrator or a teacher?

Ans. If in a nativity, Venus becomes the strongest planet with reference to the 10th Bhava, and occupies powerful places from Lagna and the Moon and joins Mercury, the native becomes an engineer.

If the lord of the 10th occupies Katakamsa (Cancer Navamsa) and is aspected or joined by Saturn, the native becomes an agricultural demonstrator.

If the 10th is occupied or aspected by Mercury or the lord of the 10th is aspected or joined by Mercury, the native becomes a teacher.

Q. 13. If the lords of the 10th and the 3rd join or aspect each other, it is said that the native will be without fortune in the Dasa of the 10th lord and he will enjoy fortunate results in the Dasa of the 3rd lord. How?

Ans. The lord of the 10th is spoiled by the aspect of the lord of the 3rd, while the lord of the 3rd is improved by the aspect of the lord of 10th. In the example of Aquarius Lagna with Mars being the lord of the 3rd and the 10th, if there is no combination or aspect of any other planet, Mars Dasa will be favourable or unfavourable according to its strength derived from position and other sources of strength.

Calculation

Q. 14. How to make use of the English calendar in calculating the solar years of the Dasas and Bhuktis in a horoscope?

Ans. The nature of a year in Dasas, i.e. its duration is a controversial point. Arguments are advanced to show that a Dasa year is so far, by some, as lunar by others, sidereal, Sayana, etc., by yet others all with equal force. Here I shall give a simple method to make use of the English calendar which will serve our purpose. Suppose a Dasa Bhukti begins on 1-1-1948, say Sun Dasa Venus Bhukti which lasts one year. If the astronomical year is taken, the last day of the Bhukti should be 31-12-1948. But in the usual method of calculation it ends with 26-12-1948, and the next Dasa, i.e., of Moon will be deemed to begin from 27-12-1948., Thus for each year, the Dasa and Bhukti will run forward at the rate of about 5 days for each year and 21 days for 4 years. It will be necessary to subtract this period from the result obtained in the calculation to secure the actual Dasa and Bhukti in operation according to the astronomical method from which the date of the English calendar can be ascertained easily, e.g., suppose Saturn Dasa Jupiter Bhukti ends with the 20th year of the native by the usual calculation. The calculation will be as follows: 20 years minus (5x 21 days) = 20 years - 105 days or 3 months and 15 days. Result: 19 years, 8 months and 20 days. Add this to the date of birth and that will give the actual date of the English calendar when Saturn Dasa Jupiter Bhukti will end.

Q. 15. On what basis is Garbha Sishta (balance of Dasa at birth) calculated? Is not the expired portion regarded as finished in the womb of the mother?.

Ans. Certainly not. The expired portion of the Dasa is supposed to be based on the last Dasa of the native in his previous birth. When the native dies, he completes a certain portion of the Dasa. The 'Garbha Sishta Dasa' is only a continuation from the point it left off in its previous birth. It has nothing to do with the period of the child in the womb or the age of its mother. Beings are born and reborn to enjoy their 'Karmaphala' which are indicated by the Dasas. The term 'Garbha Sishta Dasa' is a misnomer for 'Karma Sishta Dasa'.

Q. 16. Which system of Dasa is advisable as there are several systems given in different treatises?

Ans. Most of the Dasas mentioned by Parasara are effective in result. He holds that when the Sun is strong, Pindayurdasa should be followed; when the Moon is strong, adopt Naisargika Dasa; when Mars is strong, take up Bhinnashta Varga Dasa; when Mercury is the strongest, take Rasmi Dasa. Where Jupiter, is so, take Nakshatra Dasa. When Venus is strong, do Kalachakra Dasa. When Saturn is the strongest, take up Samudaya Ashtakavarga Dasa. Dasas based on Jaimini are too short for easy grasping only two chapters have been explained by ancient and medieval writers. Arudha Dasa can be adopted when the Navamsa chart is stronger than the Rasi Chakra.

Q. 17. (a) In Vimshottari, as well as Ashtottari system, the period of Dasas differs from planet to planet. What is the standpoint of these divisions?

(b) Why is Ketu unrepresented in Astottari?

Ans. Unfortunately, the great Rishis did not give the reasons. They might have had their own reasons, though they are not recorded in any of their writings.

Q. 18. How to calculate the Dasas when the duration of star varies below and above 60 ghatis.

Ans. The duration of a star is always dependent upon the time taken by the Moon to traverse an arc of 13° 20' in the ecliptic circle. The Moon being a very unsteady planet does not have a uniform rate of motion. Any almanac will give you the duration of stars. The Dasa period assigned to a planet is in respect of the time taken by the Moon for passing through the constellation ruled by the said planet and not on the 60 ghatis constant. When the duration of the Nakshatra and the time yet to elapse (in the nakshatra) at the time of birth are known, then the Dasa balance can be obtained thus, The duration of the star: the time yet to elapse: the Dasa period: balance of Dasa.

Q. 19. Are we to take 360 days or 365¼ days in calculating Dasas?

Ans. In calculating a year, we have five different methods: Soura, Savana, Nakshatra, Chandra and Barhaspathya. Soura-365¼ days; Savana-360 days; Nakshatra-324 days; Chandra-354 days; and Barhaspathya-365 days.

In Dasa calculation whether we have to follow Soura or Savana is a thorny question even among the great Rishis.

Garga[1] is of opinion that for Ayurdaya (longevity) and Prayaschitta (propitiations) Savana reckoning should be considered. Bhattotpala is of opinion[2] that in first Dasas and, Bhuktis one has to take into account Savana calculations (एवं पुरुषस्य जन्म). From these, we see that Savana calculation has to be looked into.

Mantreswara is of opinion that Soura or solar reckoning may be employed.

---

1 आयुर्दीय विभागश्च प्रायश्चित क्रिया तथा।
   सावने नैव कर्तव्य: सत्राणामप्युपासनम्।।

2 मयो सावनमहर्गणं कृत्वा तस्यन्तिथि नक्षत्रच्छेदं।
   तत्कालिकं कृत्वा तथा दशान्तर्दशा: कार्या: तत: आगमादिं दशदित्वं वक्तव्यं।।

Here Mantreswara recommends[1] Soura Varsha. Both these views cannot be brushed aside. Some are of the opinion that, as Garga and Bhattotpala dealt with Pindayurdaya and other Dasantardasas, Savana calculation must not be applied to Ududasas. That Savana calculation must be used only for Pindayurdasas, Bhattotpala the commentator of Varahamihira or the Great Rishi Garga, says nowhere. On the contrary, both these authors have not condemned the application of Ududasa anywhere. Bhattotpala has praised Parasara, the originator of Ududasa. From this we have to conclude that both Garga and Bhattotpala want that Savana calculation should be followed for all Dasas.

Q. 20. Some astrologers say that the Vimshottari system is not applicable in Sind and Gujarat. Instead, the Ashtottari system prevails there. How far is this true?

Ans. There is no Rishi Prokta (Rishi's injunction) exempting Sind and Gujarat from the Vimshottari system. Parasara makes no such injunction. As in medicine so in astrology, there are many methods and a careful astrologer will weigh all aspects and adopt one. South Indian astrologers may say that Ashtottari is not, their Desacbara and this does not mean that the system is inapplicable.

Yogas

Q. 21. Reconcile the following statements:

(a) A malefic combining with a benefic reduces the benefic effect of the latter; (b) a malefic combining with a malefic acquires its evil effect. But Saturn and Jupiter, Moon-Saturn, Moon-Mars and Venus-Saturn conjunctions and

---

1 रविस्फुटस्तज्जनने यदासीत् तथाविधश्चेत् गतिवर्षमर्कः।
आवृत्तयस्सन्ति दशाब्दकानां भागक्रमन्तदिवस: प्रकल्प्या:॥

combinations like Saturn-Mars, Saturn-Rahu, Mars-Rahu, etc., confer yogas.

Ans. Three separate notions as to the disposition of planets, friendly or otherwise should be considered. (1) First, there is what is called, inherent benefic and malefic disposition i.e., some planets are natural benefics like Jupiter, Venus, waxing Moon and well-associated Mercury. Natural malefics are Saturn, Mars, Sun, Rahu and Ketu, etc. This nature is to be taken note of in ordinary planetary conjunctions and aspects. (2) This inherent nature is altered for some purposes by ownership of Bhavas. Malefics owning Kendras becomes auspicious for particular purposes, and benefics owning Kendras become just the opposite. Ownership of Trikonas is good for all planets. When malefics become completely auspicious by ownership of a Kendra and Trikona at the same time, e.g., Saturn for Libra and Taurus, they are termed Yogakarakas and by themselves confer one type of yoga called Raja Yoga. Even here if the yogakaraka is in conjunction with an unfriendly planet and a malefic, such as Sun, his good effects will be correspondingly reduced. (3) The conjunctions, oppositions, etc., of inherent malefics are as a rule bad and the conjunction of a malefic with a benefic ordinarily affects the nature of the latter adversely. This always holds good. Certain yogas relate to such combinations and they are classed separately, and are treated as beyond the scope of the ordiriary rules. In this there are good yogas as well as bad yogas: The genius of interpretation of Hindu Astrology largely consists of recognising, correlating and synthesising such yogas in the judgment of a horoscope after carefully appraising their strength. Though the combinations which technically constitute yoga are present, not all yogas take effect to the same extent and in the same manner. A strict individualization of the peculiar positions present in each horoscope is imperative.

Q. 22. Can one Rishta Bhanga Yoga destroy all the Rishtas of a child?

Ans. No. All Rishta Bhanga Yogas cannot destroy all Rishtas. They can only modify the evils caused by planets said to have produced the evil. Some authors hold that Jupiter can destroy all arishtas. They say that certain yogas can even nullify Kemadruma. In all these matters, we have to be guided by the Upadesa of our Guru (preceptor).

Q. 23. If the Sun, Venus and Saturn join in one Rasi (sign) it is Daridra Yoga. But for persons born in Taurus etc., this may bring in Raja Yoga. How do you reconcile the two?

Ans. The first is caused by the simple combination of planets as such only karaka qualities are taken into consideration. Raja Yoga is caused by the lordship of planets. As such, both will happen the first throughout life and the 2nd in Dasa periods. We have many instances of unfortunate men in the political field.

Q. 24. What are the combinations for lunacy?

Ans. There are many combinations for lunacy, and I shall give here a few of them: Mars in the 7th and Jupiter in the 1st; Saturn in the 1st and Mars in the 5th, the 7th or the 9th; and Jupiter and Saturn in the 12th.

Q. 25. Which will cause surgical operations Mars in the 8th or Ketu in the 8th?

Ans. The mere presence of a malefic planet in the 8th does not cause an operation. If Saturn is lord of Lagna and he is in the 8th aspected by Mars and Saturn aspects the 6th lord then the native will undergo an operation, especially nasal. Any malefic in any house, if further afflicted, will cause the subject to undergo operations. For example, Rahu in the 12th, aspected by Mars the 12th being Aries rendered the native to be operated upon for an ulcer in the foot. Thus, the exact seat of operation should be ascertained by a careful consideration of the point of focus of the evil influences of planets and if such a seat receives the aspect of Mars then there will certainly be an operation.

Q. 26. The Sun is the indicator of general health. The Ascendant also indicates health. Which planetary combinations give rise to ringworm, white patches and eczema?

Ans. Medical Astrology is still in an experimental stage. With the advance of modern civilisation, the number of diseases and complications are also increasing. Therefore no definite combinations can be given for the several diseases which humanity is heir to. Each planet governs one of the three humours or thridoshas. According to Ayurveda, the entire human activities are controlled by the three important forces - Vatha (wind), Pitta (bile) and Sleshma (phlegm). Therefore the general physical disposition of an individual depends upon the nature of the most powerful planet and the particular sign occupied by it and the period of suffering is denoted by the Dasas and Bhuktis of such a planet. The Sun rules bile, the Moon wind and phlegm, Mars-bile, Mercury-all the three dhatus (humours), Jupiter-phlegm, Venus-wind and phlegm and Saturn-wind. The strongest planet can be found by the method given in GRAHA AND BHAVA BALAS. Ringworm is generally caused by Mars-Rahu affliction in a place of maraka. All skin diseases are almost always caused by this combination. If the Moon is afflicted by Saturn (particularly in Aries) and Mars has also influence over the Moon, the native suffers from white patches on the skin and the like. Though Mars-Ketu conibination is spoken of favourably by standard writers-association of these two planets in Scorpio or Scorpio happening to be Lagna and receiving the combined aspect will produce complaints like eczema.

Q. 27. How to predict the following diseases astrologically: (a) cancer, (b) atrophy, (c) hernia, (d)

syphillis, (e) jaundice, (f) plethora, (g) epilepsy and (h) elephantiasis?

Ans. Unfortunately, some of these diseases are not mentioned in our ancient astrological works, though they have been detailed in medical treatises. However the following material is gathered from ancient sources:

(a) Cancer: Cancer (Kataka) stands for Cancer. When the lord happens to be the lord of the 6th or the 8th and afflicted, the native will suffer from cancer. When the Moon is afflicted by malefics being aspected by or associated with the lord of the 6th or the 8th, the native will have cancer.

(b) Atrophy: Kemadruma Yoga brings in atrophy. When the lord of 2nd happens to be a malefic and occupies or aspects the 6th, atrophy is caused. Weak benefics also bring in atrophy. When the 8th is occupied by Saturn, atrophy may result. When the lord of the 8th is weak and occupies the 6th, the 8th or the 12th atrophy is caused.

(c) Hernia (rupture): Ketu and Mars govern hernia. When they are afflicted by malefics or when they occupy the 6th or the 8th rupture is caused. Scorpio (Vrischika) governs hernia. Some consider that Pisces governs it. This has to be accepted since Ketu is the lord of Pisces. When these signs are afflicted, hernia is caused.

(d) Syphillis: Venus stands for syphillis. Virgo governs the same disease. When Venus happening to be the lord of the 6th or posited in the 6th is afflicted, he will suffer from syphillis. When Virgo happens to be the 6th house and is similarly afflicted, one will have syphillis.

(e) Jaundice: When the lord of the 2nd or the Moon is afflicted by the lord of the 6th or when the 2nd house is afflicted by the lord of the 6th being Moon, he will have jaundice.

(f) Plethora: When the 6th or 8th house happens to be a Jala Rasi (watery sign) or when the lords of these happen to be weak or afflicted and occupy Dusthanas (evil houses) plethora is caused. When Lagna is occupied by a weak watery planet and aspects the 8th house, plethora is caused. (Here partial aspect should also be looked into.)

(g) Epilepsy (fits): This disease comes under Apasmara, and readers will do well to refer to PRASNA MARGA, Chapter III Here care must be taken to see whether the native's Lagna is afflicted by Upagrahas as Dhuma; then the yogas will come true.

(h) Elephantiasis: Capricorn (Makara) stands for this disease. Saturn governs the same. When afflicted Capricorn happens to be the 6th or Saturn is associated with Rahu or Ketu or when he aspects the 6th along with malefics, the native will have elephantiasis.

Here the 6th house alone has been taken into consideration. The 8th house also may be included. Further, in affirming both the nature of the disease and its prevalence, Upagrahas play a prominent part. Though Gulika alone is generally considered, others also must be examined.When they afflict the 6th or the 8th house the disease may be affirmed.

Q. 28. How to predict whether one will undergo imprisonment?

Ans. When the Sun or the Moon, weak or debilitated, occupies the 8th house and has some connection with the 6th house, there will be imprisonment. Mars too will bring in imprisonment. Strong Saturn will bring in only political imprisonment. If the 8th house is weak or afflicted or when Simhavalokana happens in Kalachakradasa, there will be imprisonment. The Dasa periods of the weak or debilitated lord of the 8th is a period of prison life.

Q. 29. How to predict the place, number of persons and relatives that will be present at the time of death?

Ans. Just as Lagna indicates birth, the 8th house indicates death. Just as you predict the number of persons present at the time of birth, calculating the same from Lagna Rasi to Chandra Lagna Rasi, you have to study the planets that are between the 8th and Chandra Rasi (the natal Moon).

There are exceptions to this rule, unnatural deaths and deaths in a battle-field. These have to be studied from the yogas present in the horoscope.

Q. 30. How to predict post mortem of the human body after death?

Ans. If there are yogas in the horoscope pointing to suspicious deaths or yogas indicating no proper samskara after death, predict post-mortem.

Q. 31. When the lord of the 1st who is also the lord of the 8th is in conjunction with Ayushkaraka Saturn and Ketu and is aspected by Rahu will it shorten the life of the native?

Ans. This yoga alone cannot shorten life. When there are other combinations granting life, we have to weigh the strength of these and then come to a conclusion.

Q. 32. There are many Balarishta Yogas which are impossible to keep in memory for an ordinary astrologer. Is there any simple rule for finding out the same?

Ans. (i) Look at the Moon and Jupiter. If these are in undesirable positions there is Balarishta. (ii) If Lagna is afflicted, there is Balarishta. (iii) If the 6th, the 8th and the 12th are occupied by malefics there is Balarishta.

Q. 33. How to predict death by sun-stroke and lightning?

Ans. The weak Sun in the 8th in malefic houses not aspected by benefics will bring in sun-stroke. Weak Mars in the 8th in malefic houses not aspected by benefics will bring in death by lightning.

Q. 34. There are many methods given for calculating longevity. All of them do not give the same number of years. Which method is the best and the most reliable?

Ans. We cannot rule out one method as correct and another as wrong on the assumption that there is difference in the number of years. Parasara in his treatise wants us to follow different methods according to the strength of the planets. When the Sun is strong, Pindayurdaya is to be followed. When the Moon is strong, Naisargika Dasa is to be followed. When Mars is strong, Bhinnashtakavarga Dasa is to be followed. When Mercury is strong, Rasmi Dasa is to be followed. When Jupiter is strong, Nakshatra Dasa is to be followed. When Venus is strong, Chakra Dasa is to be followed. When Saturn is strong, Samudaya Ashtakavarga Dasa is to be followed. When Amsa is strong, Amsaka Dasa is to be followed. The reader will do well to refer to Parasara for further information in the matter. The Rasi Dasas as mentfoned in JAIMINI SUTRAS are applicable at all times and in all cases provided the strength of the Bhavas exceeds a certain limit. Here the strength has to be calculated according to Jaimini.

Q. 35. Does fifth Dasa generally cause death?

Ans. Ancient Rishis, when locating maraka periods in the Vimshottari Dasa, opined that the 3rd, the 5th and the 7th Dasas from Dasa ruling at birth should be considered as maraka or equivalent to a maraka. To assure this result other factors have to be looked into: (1) Whether other Udu Dasas end or begin concurrently ;(2) whether the Dasanatha (Dasa-lord) is weak or afflicted; (3) whether he has the ownership of the 8th or the 12th; (4) whether he is marred by Nava Doshas. It is only after carefully considering these factors death should be predicted. The 5th Dasa as such could bring about death.

Q. 36. Is death possible in the Dasa or Antardasa of Lagnadhipati ?

Ans.When the lord of the 1st is debilitated or is in Mrityu Amsa and is posited in maraka places (2nd and 7th), he may bring about death.

Q. 37. What makes one blind, lame, with large eyes, with big head and lean body?

Ans. Several combinations have been given in our texts for the different deformities mentioned above, but we shall give some yogas. If the Sun and Rahu occupy Lagna and Mars and Saturn are posited in trines, the native becomes blind. If the Moon occupies the Sun's Hora and is aspected by Saturn, the native becomes lame.If the lord of the 2nd or the Sun and the Moon occupy Scorpio, Virgo, Leo and Libra, either in Rasi or in Amsa, the native has large eyes. The lord of the Lagna occupying any one of the signs mentioned above and the Moon occupying his own Navamsa with the Sun make the native lean with a large head.

Q. 38. How to predict whether one will have the habit of stealing?

Ans. Such matters as stealing, adultery, illegitimate issue, etc., require very careful examination. Most of the treatises deal with such matters in a general way though there are many Apavada Yogas (exceptions) not mentioned therein. Ordinarily, if the 10th house has more saturnine Vargas (Saturn's sub-divisions) and Saturn is: weak, the 6th house (house of thief) has more saturnine Vargas and is connected with the 10th, we can boldly say that the native will take to stealing. Stealing is a very general word and may range from pilfering to high-way robbery. As such Rahu Yoga may be considered as pilfering and Mars Yoga as high-way robbery.

Q. 39. How to predict whether one will be addicted to drinking?

Ans. Scorpio Rasi governs intoxicants. Neecha (debilitated) Venus or Saturn also governs the same. When Scorpio happens to be the 8th house or the 3rd house and Venus or Saturn occupies an afflicted position, the native will be addicted to intoxicants.

Q. 40. What are the effects of Bhrigu Mangala Yoga for a girl born in Aries with Venus in the 2nd or the 7th? What will counteract this evil in a boy's horoscope?

Ans. The conjunction of Mars and Venus in the 2nd or the 7th for a girl, born in Aries Lagna, cannot do any harm. Mars is the lord of the 1st and the 8th and Venus is the lord of the 2nd and the 7th. Aries is the Moolakshetra for Mars and Libra for Venus. As such according to Mantreswara the lordship or Moolakshetra alone will prevail. Here Mars is the lord of the Ist and Venus is the lord of the 7th. Their combination in the 2nd or the 7th will only improve marital comfort. Plurality of wives will not occur. It is true that Mars is a malefic by nature but lordship of the 1st has made him a first class benefic. Though the lordship of the 7th for Venus a natural benefic is bad, his position in the 7th will considerably strengthen his position and cause benefic yogas. The conjunction of these in the 2nd may not be as good as the above, still a natural benefic and lord of the 2nd in conjunction with the lord of the 1st posited in the 2nd house causes Dhana, Vakpati and Samgeeta Yogas.

Q. 41. . If Mars occupies the 1st, the 4th, the 7th, the 8th or the 12th, the chart is said to have Kuja Dosha. Will this be effective if the above mentioned houses are his Swakshetra (own), Uccha (exalted) or if he is aspected by benefics?

Ans. The intensity of Angaraka Dosha (Kuja or Martian affliction) will not be felt in the cases referred to. The aspecting benefic must be strong and the houses free from other sources of affliction.

Q. 42. How is the horoscope of a person affected when (1) the lord of the 1st is Astangata (combust), (2) when the lord of the 8th is Astangata; (3) when both are in Astangata being in their own Rasi, in Uccha (exaltation) or in Neecha (debilitation) Rasis?

Ans. Both the lords of the 1st and the 8th should be strong for long life. The only difference between them is the lord of the 1st becomes strong for good in Kendras while the other does evil only. Moudhya comes under 'Avastha' or planetary state. It will be giving 'Vikala' or 'baala' (infant) effects. Uccha or Neecha comes under Sthana Bala. An Uccha planet may be in Astangata; then all the Uccha effects will exist but they will not be experienced by the native in his native land or if at all he will experience it a little. (a) If the lord of the 1st is Uccha and Astangata, he will be a king but will be banished by his subjects. (b) If the lord of the 1st is Neecha and Astangata, he will be a beggar in a foreign land. (c) If the lord of the 8th is Uccha and Astangata, he will die in peace in a foreign land after a long life. (d) If the lord of the 8th is Neecha and Astangata, he will die in a foreign land in abject poverty and misery and disease. (e) Saturn as the lord of the 8th in Neecha and Astangata indicates death in prison for serious thefts. (f) Mars as the lord of the 8th in Neecha and Astangata indicates death by hanging or gunshot for capital crimes.

In this way, study Swakshetra (own house) also. It is also a Sthana Bala. When we calculate Bala Pinda, we do not include 'Moudhya' as such though it is included in Chesta Bala.For Ayurdaya 'Moudhya' is included though views differ regarding the planets that are excluded from Moudhya Harana.

Q. 43. (a) Planets are said to be at war when they are in the same degree in the same Rasi, and the planets vanquished in a planetary fight will be inauspicious. Supposing the lords of the 9th and the 10th are in the same degree in a Rasi what result will accrue?

Ans. Planetary fights are caused by a combination of Thara-planets with Mars. Sangama is caused by a conjunction of planets with the Sun. (Thara-planets are Mars, Mercury, Jupiter, Venus and Saturn.) If the lords of the 9th and the 10th happen to be Thara-planets and one of them be Mars, and they occupy the same degree in a Rasi there will be a planetary fight. In the fight, one of them will be defeated. The vanquished planet can be understood by a number of external signs. The defeated planet will not be able to do any good. Hence the conjunction of the lords of the 9th and the 10th in a state of war and the defeat of one of them will destroy the Rajayoga.

Q. 44. What planetary combinations and karaka planets cause (a) exile, (b) incognito existence?

Ans. The 12th house generally governs exile. Saturn in the 12th in Aries aspected by Mars causes forcible exile.

Saturn in the 12th in Aries aspected by the Sun in conjunction with other malefics denotes forcible exile.

Mars in the 12th in Cancer with Saturn in Aries causes religious exile.

Incognito existence is to be predicted by planet in combustion occupying the 6th, the 8th or the 12th houses. If the lord of the 1st is weak and is in combustion and occupies the 6th, the 8th or the 12th, Ajnatavasa can be told.

Q. 45. If the lord of the 6th is debilitated and lord of the 10th is exalted, does it constitute Jaya Yoga?

Ans. When the lord of the 6th is Neecha (debilitated) and lord of the 10th is in deep exaltation Jaya Yoga is formed.

Q. 46. Define Kahala and Parvata Yogas.

Ans. Kahala Yoga: Lords of the 4th and the 9th houses should be in kendras from each other and the lord of Lagna should be strongly disposed. Kahala is also caused when the 4th lord is exalted or in his own house being conjoined with or aspected by the lord of the 10th. Both the definitions of Kahala Yoga mentioned above assume the strength of Lagna, the 4th and the 9th houses.

Parvata Yoga: Benefics being disposed in Kendras, the 6th and the 8th houses should either be unoccupied or occupied by benefic planets. For details refer to THREE HUNDRED IMPORTANT COMBINATIONS.

Q. 47. The conjunction of kendradhipati (quadrangular lord) and konadhipati (trinal lord) produce Raja Yoga. Is this yoga life-long or is it ascribed to certain periods?

Ans. The total life of the native is first called out and divided into three parts-youth, middle age and old age. The yoga will manifest in any of the three periods mentioned above or throughout life according to the position of Jupiter (vide BRIHAT JATAKA, Chapter 5).

Q. 48. Is there Kalasarpa Yoga in Mussolini's horoscope?

Ans. There is no doubt Kalasarpa Yoga in Mussolini's horoscope[1]; but the evil is tempered because the planets are hemmed in not between Rahu and Ketu but between Ketu and Rahu. Mussolini has a powerful Sula Yoga (one of the Nabhasa Yogas), because all the 7 planets are concentrated in the three houses-the 7th, the 8th and the 9th. This is quite unfavourable and will have a very adverse effect especially that Saturn is at present transiting Mussolini's Janma Rasi, in which are placed Saturn and Mars.

Q. 49. Kemadruma is said to engender misery and poverty throughout life and neutralise all benefic yogas.If there are no planets in the 2nd or the 12th from the Moon,

---

1 Lagna-Scorpio; 6th-Rahu; 7th Mars, Saturn, and the Moon; 8th-Jupiter and Venus; 9th-the Sun and Mercury; and 12th-Rahu.

Kemadruma results. If there are planets, 'Karthari Yoga' takes place. Which is better?

Ans. Kemadruma is cancelled (a) if there are planets in the kendras (quadrants) of the Moon or if the Moon is in a kendra; (b) If the Moon or Venus aspected by Jupiter occupies kendra houses or if the Moon conjoins with good planets or is hemmed in between two good planets aspected by Jupiter; (c) If the Moon is exalted, occupies his own house, or friendly house or has subha-vargas or has the full aspect of Jupiter. Karthari Yoga caused by good planets is distinctly better.

Q. 50. How do debilitated planets get their Neecha Bhanga (cancellation of debility)? What are the general and special rules to find out the same?

Ans. Debilitated planets get their Neecha Dosha removed in four ways. (a) If the lord of the sign occupied by the debilitated planet or the lord of the Rasi wherein the debilitated planet has its exaltation, occupies a quadrant from the Ascendant or the Moon. (b) If the lord of the Navamsa of the debilitated planet occupies a quadrant or a trine from the Moon, and the Moon and Lagna happens to be in Chara or movable signs or Lagna Navamsa happens to be movable. (c) If two or three or four planets happen to be, debilitated but occupy good Shashtyamsas or favourable and good Navamsas or exalted Navamsas, the evil arising from debilitation will not come to pass. (d) If the debilitated planet has good Ashtakavarga strength then again the same can be told. Only when the planet has no varga strength (Sapthavargas as hora, etc.), the evils arising from that source will afflict the native.

Q. 51. What is meant by "Kalasarpa Yoga"? Explain its effects.

Ans. Kalasarpa Yoga is formed by the situation of all planets and Lagna within Rahu and Ketu. Here Rahu must be considered as moving in an anti-clockwise direction (apasavya).

This should not be confused with "Sarpa Yoga" given by all great Rishis as being formed by the presence of Saturn in one of the Kendras, Mars in another Kendra, and the Sun in another without any association with benefics. Both these yogas are Arishta Yogas. The first Kalasarpa will have its effects, - nullified if one of the planets especially Mercury is exalted and occupies a favourable strong position or Lagna is outside Rahu and Ketu. As this yoga is not mentioned prominently by such great writers as Varaha Mihira or Satyacharya, we have to take it that it is not very effective in Kali Yuga.

Q. 52. What is Sakata Yoga, Badhaka-dhipa and Kendradhipatya Dosha?

Ans. Sakata Yoga is of two kinds: (1) The Moon in the 6th, the 8th or the 12th from Jupiter which is posited in non-kendra houses. (2) All the planets occupying the 1st and the 7th. Both these are malefic yogas.

Badhakadhipa: Badha houses are of two types: (1) Samanya badha (ordinary affliction) and (2) Visesha badha (special affliction). The 7th house and the planets posited in it are a badha (tormentors) for a common sign and the planets in it. In the same way the 9th is a badha for a fixed sign and the 11th, for a movable sign.

Visesha Badha: Aquarius is a badha for all movable signs. Scorpio is a badha for Leo, Virgo, Scorpio and Sagittarius. Capricorn is a badha for Taurus, Cancer for Aquarius , and Sagittarius for Gemini and Pisces.

Kendradhipatya Doshas: When examining Nakshatra Dasa, adhipatya dosha (affliction due to ownerships) has to be looked into. Benefics owning Kendras are weak and produce evil, while malefics owning them are strong and produce only good.

Q. 53. Just as we have 'Neechabhanga Yogas' have we not Uccha Bhanga Yogas?

Ans. Uccha Bhanga is bad; but 'Neechabhanga' is good. When an Uccha planet is aspected by another Uccha planet, the native heads for bankruptcy. Here we have 'Uccha Bhanga'.

Q. 54. If in a horoscope both Hamsa Yoga and Kemadruma are found, what will be the result?

Ans. Both these will be experienced by the native. Hamsa Yoga will be felt in the Dasa and Bhukti of Jupiter; while Kemadruma will be felt in the periods of the Moon. Some view that both these yogas will be felt throughout life, but according to BRIHAT JATAKA, these yogas happen only in their Dasa periods.

Q. 55. (a) Is it not necessary that all the benefics should be placed in the 6th, the 7th and the 8th from the Moon to form Adhi Yoga?

(b) Will the yoga be formed even if one or two of these be so situated?

(c) Will the combination or aspect of the evil planets cancel this yoga?

Ans. If all benefics occupy the 6th, the 7th and the 8th, Adhi Yoga is caused. If malefics conjoin these places, Adhi Yoga will be mixed in character. If however malefics alone occupy the 6th, the 7th and the 8th, the effects will be exactly the reverse. According to classical terms, if the benefics are weak, the native becomes a king; if the Moon is weak, the native will become a commander-in-chief; if the Moon is moderate in strength, he becomes a minister. Further all those who are born in this yoga are supposed to be happy, free from disease and enemies and long-lived. On the contrary, if all the malefics occupy the 6th, the 7th and the 8th, he will be unhappy, sickly and surrounded by foes and short lived. Our book THREE HUNDRED IMPORTANT COMBINATIONS will make the matter very clear.

Q. 56. What is the effect of Parivarthana (Exchange) Yoga of two Neecha (debilitated) planets?

Ans. Parivarthana Yogas of two strong planets holding benefic lordships are very good. Parivarthana Yogas of two planets-one Neecha and the other strong holding benefic lordship are mixed in nature; fair for the strong and bad for the weak. Parivarthana of two neecha planets both holding Dusthanas are fair. Parivarthana of two neecha planets-one holding Dusthana and the other Susthana-is bad for Susthana. In this way apply for all cases.

Q. 57. Discuss Kemadruma Yoga.

Ans. It is true that where there are no planets (Sun accepted) on either side of the Moon, Kemadruma Yoga is formed. There are also other combinations that bring in Kemadruma.

(a)When the Moon occupies Lagna or the 7th without the aspect of Jupiter, (b) When the Moon conjoins with the Sun aspected by a debilitated planet, and occupies a debilitated Navamsa. (c) When birth is in the night time, the 8th liouse from the Moon is aspected or occupied by an evil planet. (d) When the Moon is in conjunction with Rahu, and is aspected by a malefic. More combinations may be given and the readers are referred to Jataka Sarwaswa.

The Kemadruma Bhanga Yogas are: (a) Garga is of opinion that when quadrants from the Moon are occupied by planets other than the Sun, we have cancellation. (b) Some are of opinion that when the Moon is aspected by all other planets we have cancellation (Sambhu Hora). (c) Some authors as Sruthakeerthi or Jeevasarma state, when Thara planets occupy both sides of the Moon's Navamsa, there is no Kemadruma. This has not been accepted by Varaha Mihira.

In all these, we have to note that the bhanga takes place only in the Dasa periods of planets causing bhanga. In the Moon Dasa, Kemadruma Yoga will be experienced.

Q. 58. Planets in their own sign or exaltation in a kendra form Pancha Mahapurusha Yoga. If such planets become malefic by ownership, what results are to be expected in the periods of such planets?

Ans. Pancha Mahapurusha Yoga is one which is experienced throughout life irrespective of Dasa or Antardasa periods. But the yoga must be strong; otherwise it will be felt only in dreams.If the yoga is weak and afflicted, results will be according to lordship only.

Q. 59. Will there be Neechabhanga in a case where the planet capable of causing Neechabhanga is also Neecha (debilitated)?

Ans. No, the Neechabhanga planet must be sufficiently strong- There are other sources of strength and if the planet is otherwise strong, there will be Neechabhanga.

Q. 60. Conjunction of lords of Dusthanas (evil houses) in Dusthanas produces Vipareetha Rajayoga. Planets in Dusthanas cannot give good results. How do you reconcile this?

Ans. Vipareetha Rajayoga cannot give good results. If he means Vichitra Rajayoga, it is a yoga caused by the presence of all the lords of Dusthanas in Dusthanas. Such pure yogas very seldom happen as lords of Dusthanas will also be lords of good houses.

Q. 61. Kindly define the following:

(a) Parvata Yoga, (b) Kahala, (c) Sree Yoga.

Ans. (a) Parvata Yoga is of 6 different kinds: (i) When benefic planets occupy kendras, the 6th and the 8th houses contain benefics or are free from malefic planets; (ii) when the lords of the 1st and the 12th occupy quadrants from each other aspected by a friendly planet;(iii) when the lords of the 1st and the 12th occupy quadrants in friendly houses aspected by non-retrograde planets; (iv) when the lord of the house occupied by the lord of the 7th is in a quadrant, trine, or Moolatrikonas; (v) when both the lords of the 2nd and the 11th occupy their exaltation houses; (vi) when benefic planets occupy the 7th, malefics occupy the 2nd and the lord of the 11th is connected with malefics.

(b) Kahala Yoga: There are many types of Kahala Yogas. (i) When the lords of the 9th and the 4th occupy mutual kendras and the lord of the 1st is strong; (ii) when the lord of the 4th either in conjunction with, or aspected by, the lord of the 10th occupies exaltation or own house; (iii) when the lord of the 4th occupies kendras or Moolatrikona or Uccha;. (iv) when the lord of the 1st is strong, the lords of the 4th and the 10th being friendly to each other occupy kendras; (v) when the Navamsa lord of Lagnadhipa combines with any planet in exaltation and Lagnadhipa occupies his house of exaltation; (vi) when benefics and malefics occupy the 9th, the Sun and Saturn occupy the 10th and the lord of the 1st is strong and in common Rasis; (vii) the Navamsa lord of the 1st occupies in conjunction with a benefic lord his house of exaltation in a quadrant; (viii) when the lords of the 4th and the 8th exchange houses or combine in kendras; (ix) the Navamsa lord of the lord of the 9th is aspected by benefics or is in subha vargas; (x) when the lord of the 1st or the 9th occupies Uccha or Moolatrikona;(xi) when Saturn in Vargottama occupies Uccha or Moolatrikona; (xii) when Mercury or Jupiter occupies the 7th in Uccha Rasi; (xiii) when benefics occupy kendras and when birth takes place in the night in a Chara Lagna (movable sign) aspected by Jupiter; (xiv) when Lagna is a fixed sign and the lord of the 1st is in a fixed Navamsa and when any planet occupies the 8th; (xv) when the lord of that Rasi wherein the lord of the 1st is posited is in Uccha or in a kendra house from the Moon-sign.

(c) Sree Yoga: Sree Yogas are of two kinds-Sreenatha Yoga and Sreekantha Yoga. When Lagna lord, the Sun and the moon occupy Kendras or trikonas in Uccha or Swakshetra or friendly houses, we have Sreekantha Yoga. Sreenatha Yoga: When the lord of the 9th, Mercury and Venus occupy Kendras in Uccha, Swakshetra or friendly house, we have Sreenatha Yoga.[1]

Q. 62. What are Dala, Kartari. Sakata and Dhwaja Yogas ? How are they caused?

Ans. Dala Yogas are two in number-Mala and Sarpa Yogas. When Venus, Mercury and Jupiter occupy different Kendras without being afflicted by malefics, Mala Yoga is formed. When Saturn occupies a Kendra, Mars another Kendra and the Sun in a third Kendra without association or aspect of a benefic (natural) Sarpa Yoga is formed. Dala is good, while Sarpa is bad.

SARAVALI, when discussing the general effects of Dala Yogas, states that persons born in these will prosper either through royal favour or through their own luck or through the luck of others. They will be sometimes happy and sometimes very miserable (Verse 10, Chapter 21 of SARAVALI).

Kartari Yogas: When thara grahas i.e., Mars, Mercury, Jupiter, Venus and Saturn) occupy the 2nd and the 12th from Lagna, Kartari Yogas are caused. Subha Kartari Yogas are good, while Asubhas are bad.

Sakata Yogas are of two types, viz., (a) when all planets occupy the I st and the 7th; (b) when the Moon occupies the 6th, the 8th or the 12th from Jupiter and at the same time he is outside Kendras.

Persons born in this will be happy in some periods and will be extremely miserable in certain periods of their lives.

Dhwaja Yogas: When Upagraha Indra Dhwaja occupies Kendras in conjunction with Jupiter, we have Dhwaja Yogas. This is a Raja Yoga.

---

1 See *Three Hundred Important Combinations.*

Q. 63. If a Neecha Bhanga Rajayoga occurs, will the planets, the one in debilitation and the other that cancels the debilitation become Yogakarakas?

Ans. No. Rajayoga will take place in the Dasa periods of the planets that bring about Neecha Bhanga.

Q. 64. In PHALA DEEPIKA, it is said that planets in retrogression give the same effects as if they are in exaltation. Can this be made use of in yogas as Hamsa, etc.?

Ans. It is true that the effects of Subha Vakra (benefic and retrograde) planets are as intense as those of exalted planets. But care should be taken to differentiate exaltation from Vakra or retrogression. In Hamsa and Ruchaka Yogas, exaltations alone play a part. SARAVALI is of the opinion that Asubha Vakras bring in more malefic effects only and as such 'Vakras' give strength to planets. It may be malefic or benefic.

Q. 65. What is a Yogakaraka Graha (planet)? Are the Yogakarakas fixed for every Lagna?

Ans. The term means a planet causing yoga. Though it includes strictly speaking 'bad yogas' also Parasara restricts this to certain planets for each Lagna. This classification is based on Adhipatya (lordship). For every Lagna, he enumerates certain planets and they are expected to give 'Yoga'. Yogakaraka may also include 'Paraspara Karaka' (mutual).

Q. 66. In a horoscope according to JAIMINI SUTRAS the Moon is posited in Scorpio and aspects Mars in Cancer and vice versa. Does this cause Vichitra Raja Yoga?

Ans. No. The aspect referred to applies only to all those yogas mentioned by Jaimini. Jaimini does not mention Vichitra Raja Yogas. According to general cannons of astrology, the Moon cannot aspect Mars or vice versa in these circumstances.

Q. 67. Discuss fully in the appended chart[1] (a) Whether one Neecha (debilitated planet) aspecting another Neecha makes one a beggar or a monarch?

(b) Whether there is any Rajayoga formed by the combination of the lords of kendras with the lords of trikonas?

(c) Whether it is nullified by the combination of the lord of the 11th, etc?

Ans. It is very doubtful whether one Neecha aspecting another Neecha can make one a monarch by the sheer influence of this yoga. If both have Neechabhanga and favourable in other ways good may result. Here the Sun has 'neecha bhanga' and Saturn's debilitation has been modified to a certain extent by the aspect of many planets. The aspects of the Sun in Libra and of Saturn in Aries and vice versa have been noted in SARAVALI in Chapter 22, verse 17 and in Chapter 29, verse 25. Saturn's aspect suggests that "the native does unworthy actions; he is addicted to old women. He is lazy" etc. The Sun's aspect makes him a good agriculturist with sheep-farming. Hence the Dasa periods of these mutually aspecting Neechas will give him lands, etc.

(b) The combination has produced a Rajayoga but the full effects cannot be perceived by the evils arising from ownership. Jupiter and Mercury though benefics are spoiled by their ownership. We should bear in mind that the evil effects of ownership will be perceived only in the Dasa periods and not throughout life.

Q. 68. Supposing the lords of the 6th, the 8th and the 12th are in association with one another, in any house other than the 6th, the 8th or the 12th; or they have mutual aspect; will it produce Rajayoga?

---

1   Dhanus-Lagna; the Moon-Aquarius; Saturn and Rahu-Aries; the Sun, Mercury, Venus, Mars, Jupiter and Ketu-Libra.

Ans. This combination if it produces Rajayoga seems to be strange. The lords of the 6th, the 8th and the 12th are Dhurthas and destroy wherever they are situated. Even when they are in the 6th, the 8th or the 12th they enhance the evil nature of those Bhavas. "When all planets occupy the 6th, the 8th or the 12th, they bring in a Rajayoga" (Verse 537, Chapter III, LAGHU JATAKA SARVASVA). This is also apparently strange, but this is explained by great Rishis saying the 6th, the 8th and the 12th being renunciation signs (Bandha Mochana) planets occupying them indicate "Detachment from "worldly life" and the extinction of past Karmaphala. In that sense the above yoga is a Rajayoga. Similarly the yoga mentioned in-Uttarakalamrita, Khanda IV, Sloka 22, will have to be construed in that way. Lords of detachment by their presence in "Karma-phala" Bhavas (houses which indicate the reaping of the fruits of karma) bring in detached attachment to worldly affairs, thereby paving the way for Moksha. But the verse requires careful scrutiny lest a later insertion or an improper distortion of the verse should pass for Rishi prokta or an authoritative utterance.

Q. 69. Have we Neechabhanga Rajayoga for Rahu and Ketu?

Ans. If we can have Neechabhanga Yogas for Mars, Saturn and others, I do not see why we should not extend the same to Rahu and Ketu. Parasara is very clear in declaring that Virgo is to be owned by Rahu and Pisces is to be owned by Ketu. The exaltation sign for Rahu is Taurus and for Ketu, Scorpio. Here also views differ but one that is given above is more authoritative.

Q. 70. Should yogas be reckoned from Bhavas or Rasis?

Ans. This is a most controversial question. But for the purposes of horoscopic interpretations, yogas may be said to depend upon Rasis and not on Bhavas. Chandra Yogas, Ravi Yogas and several of the Nabhasa Yogas have reference to Rasis and not Bhavas. Parasara is inclined to the view that Kendras refer to Rasis while Balabhadra the author of HORARATNA holds that Kendras refer to the 4th, the 7th and the 10th Bhavas. Parasara's view must doubtless prevail in the matter. Therefore yogas which are based on the disposition of planets in Kendras have also to be reckoned in terms of Rasi Chakra.

Q. 71. Define Pancha Mahapurusha Yoga.

Ans. Mars, Mercury, Jupiter, Venus and Saturn in a Kendra identical with its Swakshetra (own house) or Uccha (exaltation) will give rise respectively to Ruchaka Bhadra, Hamsa, Malavya and Sasa Yogas. Varaha Mihira has described the lakshanas or qualities of the five Mahapurusha Yogas in his BRIHAT SAMHITA to which further reference may be made. These yogas in order to be fully operative should be constituted without flaws, i e., the planets causing them should as usual be free from afflictions.

Q. 72. Define Chamara Yoga, Guru Chandala Yoga and Budha-Aditya Yoga.

Ans. Chamara Yoga: When an exalted lord of the 1st aspected by Jupiter occupies a quadrant, we get Charnara Yoga. In JATAKA CHINTAMANI, the following combinations are given:

(a) When the lord of the 1st conjoins Jupiter aspected by Venus and occupies the 2nd, the 5th, the 8th or the 11th.

(b) When the Lagna is Chara (moveable) and the lord of the 1st occupies the 9th or the 10th.

(c) When Lagna is aspected by Jupiter and the Navamsa lord of Jupiter occupies an exalted position.

(d) When the lord of the 1st is strong and the 3rd house or 11th house is joined by either benefics or malefics exclusively. Benefics and malefics should not join together.

(e) When the Sun is in Vargottamamsa (occupying the same sign in Navamsa), the lord of the 1st is exalted and Mercury occupies the 5th or the 9th house.

(f) When Lagna is Chara , and the lords of the 4th and the 7th are strong.

(g) When Lagna is in Chara Rasi, the lord of the 1st is in the 12th, Jupiter in a kendra, and birth occurs in Sukla Paksha (bright half).

(h) When the lord of the 1st is exalted, the lord of the 11th is in the 9th and the Ascendant is in Sthira Rasi (a fixed sign).

(i) When birth is in daytime, the Moon is strong and full and when the lord of the 1st is exalted and Lagna is conjoined by any one planet.

(j) When the Sun, Mercury and Venus occupy mutual Kendra houses.

(k) When the lord of the 1st is in Chara (moveable) Navamsa and the lord of the 10th occupies Chara Rasi, and the lord of the 4th is in the 7th.

(l) When the lord of the 1st is in the 9th, the lord of the 4th is exalted and occupies Kendra positions, and another planet joins the Kendra houses of the lord of the 4th.

Guru-Chandala Yoga: When Jupiter combines with a weak Saturn or when he joins Rahu or when he is along with Gulika, we have Guru-Chandala Yoga. Some authors take that when Jupiter becomes Gulika Bhavadhipa (lord of sign held by Gulika) or Rahu Rasyadhipa (lord of sign held by Rahu), we have Guru-Chandala Yoga. Note that in all these cases, Jupiter must be weak and debilitated.

Budha-Aditya Yoga: This is another name for Nipuna Yoga. When Murcury and the Sun join in one Rasi, we have this yoga.

Q. 73. What are the cumulative effects of Guru-Chandala Yoga? Are any remedies prescribed for neutralising the evil influences?

Ans. The cumulative effects vary with reference to the strength of Guru (Jupiter) and Rahu, the nature of the sign involved and the Bhava position. Therefore no general results can be ascribed. When the yoga is strong, and when the conjunction says is exact, the subject will have no regard for spiritual values or he will have perverted views. The conscience factor will be absent and the subject will be carried away by momentary considerations. If the combination occurs, in the 10th house, the person lacks moral courage; if in the 12th house, spiritual aspirations will be directed in wrong channels; in the 11th, the sting is removed; in Lagna, moral character will be questionable; in the 5th house, lacks consideration and there will be sorrow through children. The yoga in general does not obstruct material prosperity. Its importance is only in regard to the spiritual, moral and religious aspect of human existence. When Jupiter is strong the yoga naturally becomes defunct.No remedial measures are prescribed to alleviate the evils due to Guru-Chandala Yoga, but regular practice of Pranayama under a suitable Guru (preceptor or teacher) will doubtless act as an antidote.

Q. 74. Define: Ruchaka and Sasa Yogas will not occur in the case of Gemini Lagna births.

Ans. Ruchaka Yoga is caused by Mars occupying a Kendra identical with his own or exaltation sign. Aries and Scorpio are own houses; Capricorn is the exaltation house. These three happen to be the 12th, the 6th and the 8th from Gemini and hence Ruchaka Yoga cannot occur for Mithuna (Gemini).

Sasa Yoga is caused by Saturn occupying a kendra identical with his Uchcha (exaltation) or Swakshetras (own houses). Saturn's Uchcha is Libra; his Swakshetras are Capricorn and Aquarius. Those three signs happen to be the 5th, the 8th and the 9th and hence the impossibility of Sasa Yoga for Gemini Ascendants.

But since Pancha Maha Purusha Yoga is to be considered both from Lagna and the Janma Rasi (Moon-sign), the presence of Ruchaka and Sasa for Mithuna (Gemini) people cannot be entirely ruled out unless the Moon is also in Gemini.

Q. 75. Define hemming inbetween evil planets. Will it be papamadhyamasthiti if a planet is posited midway between two evil planets, all the three planets occupying one and the same Rasi (sign) or two Rasis, or is it necessary that three different houses should be involved for hemming? Is there any difference in effect between these?

Ans. The term 'Papamadhyasthiti' means situated between evil planets. This necessarily applies whether it takes place in a single sign or in two or three signs. But there is a difference in their practical application. The term is generally held to denote when a planet in one sign is beseiged by evil planets in both the adjacent signs. When the above happens in a single sign itself, this is classed in Hindu Astrology as conjunction which is considered more powerful than 'hemming'. When only two signs are involved, it is neither hemming nor conjunction but is considered as Dwirdwadasa.

Q. 76. What is the effect of Guru-Mangala Yoga in Capricorn on the life of a person born in Vrishabha (Taurus) Lagna?

Ans. It is true that Jupiter is in debilitation and Mars is in exaltation. Guru-Mangala Yoga ordinarily is good. The yoga here takes place in the 9th house. While dealing with Bhagya Chinta SARAVALI gives the following effects:

"The native will have landed property and wealth. He will be honoured by all. But he will be unhealthy-a prey to diseases. He will have often wounds in his body." Evidently Jupiter contributes the first part and Mars, the 2nd part.For a person born in Taurus, Mars is the lord of the 12th and the 7th. Jupiter is the lord of the 8th and the 11th. Takng all these lordships into consideration, the yoga effects cannot be good. But the association of a subha (benefic), however weak he may be, cannot spoil the effects of a strong malefic. Hence the effects cannot be totally evil also.

SARAVALI again states that, when Jupiter in Capricorn is aspected by Mars, the native will be valorous, famous, respected by all, proud and a renowned soldier. There is an old saying that when an exalted malefic combines with a debilitated benefic, the association gives good results; when a debilitated malefic combines with an exalted benefic, the combination brings in very bad results. In this particular case, good results alone have to be expected.

Q. 77. You stress upon Papakarthari Yoga and Dwirdwadasa positions as being too bad and as reducing the benefic influence of planets. In Mr. Churchill's [1]horoscope there are afflictions to his Lagna and third house where there are Papakarthari Yogas and Dwirdwadasa positions for six planets. How can you explain his rank and position in view of the above afflictions?

Ans. Papakarthari Yoga and Dwirdwadasa positions are of minor importance in the light of more powerful yogas-good and bad. A horoscope may have several Rajayogas but the native will have a checkered career if the planets causing such yogas are between malefics. So far as Dwirdwadasa is concerned the dosha plays some considerable part in directional astrology. Lords of certain Dasa and certain Bhukti if situated in the 2nd and the 12th from each other will produce decidedly malefic results. Thus the mere presence of Dwirdwadasa and Papakarthari does not lessen the value of a horoscope. if Rajayogas and other powerful combinations are present.

1 Rasi: Libra-Ascendant, Mercury and Ketu; Scorpio-the Sun; Sagittarius-Venus; Capricorn-Saturn; Aries-Rahu; Leo-the Moon; and the Virgo-Mars.

In Mr.Churhill's horoscope no doubt the Lagna and Lord of Lagna are subject to Papakartari and almost all planets are in the 2nd and the 12th from each other. A careful scrutiny of the chart will however reveal strong dispositions. According to standard astrological writers, only 4 Bhavas are important (Bhavaihi chaturbhihi balubhihi- Dhanabhagya ayakarmabhihi), viz., the 2nd, the 9th, the 11th and the 10th. These should be reckoned either from Lagna or from the Moon whichever is more powerful.

Taking from Lagna: (1) Lord of the 2nd Mars is in the 12th-bad; (2) Lord of the 9th Mercury is in Lagna-good; with Jupiter lord of the 3rd and the 6th-bad; (3) Lord of the 11th Sun is in the 2nd-very good; (4) Lord of the 10th is in the 11th-good. Then taking from the Moon: (1) Lord of the 2nd Mercury is in the 3rd with Jupiter lord of the 5th. (2) Lord of the 9th Mars is a yogakaraka and his situation in the 2nd is excellent. (3) Lord of the 11th Mercury has the same disposition as lord of the 2nd. Lord of the 10th Venus is in the 5th aspected by Mars, a yogakaraka. The 10th is aspected by the Sun who happens to be Lagnadhipati. These explain the high position which Mr. Churchill occupied. The Dwirdwadasa and Papakarthari Yogas illustrate the early struggles and experiences in Mr. Churchill's life. He had to fight through several odds to make his personality great.

Q. 78. When a number of planets make up yoga, when can the effect of this yoga be realise? For example take the yoga: "when all planets occupy Makara (Capricorn), Kumbha (Aquarius), Meena (Pisces), Mesha (Aries), Vrishabha (Taurus) and Mithuna (Gemini), the native becomes a king."

Ans. Yoga is formed by Rasis alone, or by Bbavas alone or by planets as karakas or Bhavadhipatis alone. It is also formed by the combination of any two of the above. Here

Rasis alone cause the yoga. Neither strength nor position taken individually or collectively produces this yoga. As such Dasa periods of planets need not be looked into. Its results show throughout life. Raja Yoga does not imply acquisition of kingship. It signifies only "political success". JAIMINI SUTRAS mention Dasas calculated from Rasis. Kalachakra Dasa is based on Rasis. These Rasi Dasas indicate the time of the yoga. Here we have to calculate the strength of the Rasis as mentioned in JAIMINI SUTRAS.

Q. 79. For Cancer Lagna, Jupiter and Mars are in Capricorn and Saturn is in a Kendra (quadrant) from the Moon causing the Neechabhanga (cancellation of debility) of Jupiter. When will this Yoga operate?

Ans. Here Neechabhanga is caused not by one planet alone but by both Saturn and Mars. Among these two, Mars will have the upper hand being qualified in more than one way, i.e., (a) as Thaduccbanatha in Lagna Kendra, (b) Neecha joining an Uccha planet. The yoga will manifest during the periods of Jupiter and Mars to a lesser extent in Saturn Dasa/Bhukti also.

Q. 80. (a) Is Chandramangala Yoga formed by the Moon-Mars opposition also:

(b) Do vakra (retrograde) planets enhance the qualities or show a falling off of the qualities?

Ans. (a) Chandramangala Yoga is always supposed to arise by the association of the Moon and Mars together. Nowhere has it seemed to have been authoritatively suggested that the Moon and Mars by a disposition-any other than conjunction-would cause Chandramangala.

(b) As a rule planets in vakra are said to be strong. All the five non-luminous planets are strong when they are in retrograde motion. When a planet is in retrograde motion he is supposed to produce more or less the same beneficial results as those resulting from occupation of exaltation. When a planet whose Dasa or Bhukti is current should transit through his debilitation or unfriendly house much suffering and misery would be produced. If however such a planet is vakra (retrograde), the effects will then be good. Even when calculating Ayurdaya (longevity) the Ayushkalas (quota of life-rays) contributed by a planet should be trebled if the planet is vakra. The above views are expounded by great writers. In actual practice, however, it is found that especially at time of transit, malefic planets cause such suffering, ill-health and disturbed conditions while the reverse holds good when benefics are vakra. In international affairs sometimes surprising developments will occur when Saturn and Mars are vakra.

Q. 81. Are we to take Bhava Kundali for yogas?

Ans. The above yogas are based on Bhava Kundali. Some yogas are based on Rasi positions alone and they come under Asraya Phala. This has been mentioned in their respective places in the various old treatises.

Q. 82. It is stated that when planets are situated in the latter part of the horoscope, the yoga will commence only in the latter half of life. Do you agree with this?

Ans. There is no such rule based on authority. It is said that the man who has his planets in the latter half of his chart, if they are strong and well posited, will find the latter period of his life better than the earlier part. The Dasa periods then must also be good.

Q. 83. Sun-Mercury is situated in a Kendra (quadrant) with an aspect of Jupiter as well as Mars. Does Mars spoil Budha-Aditya Yoga when Lagna is Capricorn?

Ans. In this instance Mercury and the Sun are within $3°1/3$ of each other. It is this that destroys the yoga and not the aspect of Mars as you think. Mars is not evil for Capricorn

Ascendant and his aspect will not affect the yoga adversely though he is a natural malefic. Nor does the aspect of Jupiter augment the yoga as he is inauspicious for this Lagna.

Q. 84. Are different yogas in astrology to be taken with respect to Bhavas?

Ans. Both Bhavas and Rasis play a role in forming yogas. In some yogas Bhavas alone form the yoga. In some, Rasis alone play the part. The two cannot be mixed. Yogas are formed in seven ways: Rasi position; Bhava position; the above two combined; planets and Bhavas; planets alone; Rasis, Bhavas and planets; and planets and Rasis.

(a) 'शुभ वर्गोत्तमे जन्म' etc. Here we have a yoga caused by Sthana (Vargottama Rasi). There is no reference to Bhavas or planets.

(b) 'अशून्येषु च केन्द्रेषु' etc. Here we have only Bhava and no reference to Sthana or planets.

(c) 'लग्नं मूर्द्धोदयं' Here we have reference to Bhavas and Rasis.

(d) Adhi Yoga, etc., refers only to Bhavas and planets.

(e) 'सुखिनः प्रकृष्टकार्याः' Etc. Here we have reference only to planets.

(f) Ruchaka, Bbadra, Hamsadi Yogas refer to Rasis (Sthana), Bhavas and planets.

(g) 'यातेष्वत्स्वसमयेषु दिनेशहोरा' etc. Here we have no reference to Bhavas.

Readers will do well to go through PRASNA MARGA (Chapter 9, Verses 54, 55 and 56).

Q. 85. Hamsa Yoga is said to be caused when Jupiter occupies a Kendra identical with its own or exalted house. Is it not to be considered as a Kendradhipatya Dosha?

Ans. Here we find 3 classes of Hamsa Yogas. In a Hamsa

Yoga where Jupiter is exalted no Kendradhipatya occurs which automatically becomes yoga of the 3rd degree magnitude. Next comes the yoga formed in Sagittarius or Pisces where he can be in Lagna itself and the rest are 3rd class. Even in the last case, the Kendradhipatya Dosha operates only during his Dasa periods.

Q. 86. "Mars in Cancer brings wealth." To clarify it Mr. V. S. Sastri says that bad planets in depression do good. . Does this mean (i) even as lord of the 11th, Mars in depression will bring wealth. (ii) If bad planets in depression do good, why then are Mars singled out as the giver of wealth only? What about its Bhava or Karaka effects?

Ans. BRIHAT JATAKA (16th chapter) states that Mars in Cancer brings wealth. This is only an asraya effect in Mars. It has nothing to do with Bhava or Bhavadhipatya effects. It has no reference to the house of depression but only to Cancer. As such we cannot say planets in depression bring wealth.

Muhurta

Q. 87. What are the masculine, feminine and effeminate constellations?

Ans. Masculine, feminine and effeminate constellations are those that are presided over, according to Vimshottari system, by masculine, feminine and effeminate planets respectively. For instance the Sun presides over Krittika, Uttara and Uttarashadha. Since the Sun is a masculine planet these constellations are said to be masculine ones.

Q. 88. Which are the best signs of the zodiac in which the Moon's position in the sign will help to accelerate the

germination and growth of seeds sown?

Ans. Views differ regarding this. They differ with different places and different seeds. Hence it is not possible to formulate a general rule.

(i) In South India the following is observed for sowing of seeds:

(a) Reject Aries, Scorpio, Sagittarius and Virgo Rasis (when fixing the time); (b) Reject the following constellations: 1. Jyeshta, 2. Pubba, 3. Poorvashadha, 4. Poorvabhadra, 5. Bharani, 6. Chitta, 7. Aslesha and 8. Makha ; (c) Nakshatras in Rahu Chakra, viz., the constellation wherein Rahu is posited; and (d) the 2nd, 3rd, 4th, 5th, 6th, 7th, 11th, 15th, 19th, 23rd, 24th, 25th, 26th and 27th from the constellation wherein Rahu stands.

With reference to (d): If the seed is sown in the 2nd or 3rd, crops will perish for want of water: If done in the 4th, 5th or 6th, crops will die by excess of rains or water. If done in the 7th, 11th, 15th, 19th and 23rd, crops will die by excess of rain or absence of rain, or by the troubles of mice or troublesome insects, etc. If done in the 24th, 25th, 26th or 27th, crops will grow but there will be no yield. (e) Krittika, Aridra and Visakha are neither good nor bad. These constellations have to be treated as Madhyama. (f) Sthira Karana and Khara Karana are to be rejected. Besides, Surabhi Karana and Varsha Karana have to be avoided. (g) Amongst Tithies (lunar dates), Dwiteeya (the 2nd), Saptami (the 7th), Dwadasi (the 12th), and Prathipada (the 1st) have to be set aside. (h) Amongst weekdays, leave out Tuesday and Saturday. (i) Avoid Gulika Rasi.

(ii) Regarding the planting of trees, the following rules may be observed:

(a) For coconut, arecanut, mango trees, avoid Vedha Nakshatras, Cancer, Aries and Libra Rasis.

Q. 89. Explain the importance of Vish-kambhadi

Yogas and Karanas in predictive astrology.

Ans. They are useful in Prasna and Muhurtham but in horoscopy they are useful for understanding the character of man. These 'Panchanga Yogas' can be used for examining the strength of the Moon, the Sun and Lagna and knowledge of which is absolutely essential for prediction.

Q. 90. How to predict that there are evil influences in the houses that we inhabit or own? Are we to reply on the natal horoscope alone?

Ans. I shall attempt a brief outline of the Silpi Sastra, knowledge of which is quite essential for an astrologer. Many doubts are raised regarding the nature and effects of haunted houses and houses the occupants of which suffer much either in respect of wealth or children. It is true that the nature of the building which a native will own can be answered from horoscope or prasnas; but a fuller knowledge can be gleaned only by the critical examination of the houses or mansions which persons occupy. The nature of the ground wherein the house is built may be bad, the nature of the garden that surrounds may be faulty and the nature of the construction may be against astronomical or other principles. The result is, persons who own it or occupy it suffer great privation and misery.

Silpi Sastra, the science of architecture, is as ancient as astrology and had been developed in ancient India to a marvellous accuracy which even the so-called 'moderner' cannot question. There are many treatises on the subject and readers will do well to glance through the most famous of these, viz., MANUSHYALAYA MAHA CHANDRIKA.

In the first place, before we attempt to construct a house, we should thoroughly examine the nature of the ground. Here again we have to be careful to see whether it is in a town where we have only limited space and where the rules of city construction have to be accepted. In general, it has to be stated the ground must have the following characteristics:

An ideal site must be a place where people and cows are found in large numbers, where useful trees grow, where streams flow on the right hand side, where the slope is towards the East, where the earth is hard so that the foot-steps of persons walking around can be heard at a distance, where there is plenty of water underneath, and where the quality of the earth is such that when seeds sown sprout in three days and where, when a square pit is dug and the mud is taken out, it is sufficient to refill it. The ground must also be more or less level.

A circular or semicircular or pentangular site must be rejected. Grounds resembling in shape the face of the cow, fish, elephant or tortoise must be abandoned. If the earth is full of bones, hair, or charcoal or is the abode of vermins only, it must be avoided.

If the eastern part of the ground is low and the west is high, people living in the same will prosper. When the south-east is low and the north-west is high, people living in it will suffer from loss of wealth. When the south is low, the north is high; the people living in it will die early. When the south-west is low and north-east is high, people inhabiting it will undergo all sorts of privations. The first is technically known as Co-Veethi, the 2nd Agni Veethi, the 3rd is Kala Veethi and the fourth, Bhutha Veethi.

When the west is low and east is high, inhabitants of the place will be extremely poor and suffer from the pangs of poverty. This is Vari Veethi. When the south-east is high and north-west is low, people here will lose their children. This is Sarpa Veethi. When the north is high and the south low, the inhabitants will grow rich. This is Faja Veethi. When the northeast is low, and south-west is high, people here will grow prosperous. This is Dhanya Veethi. When the inhabitants live in a ground where the middle part is low, they will have to migrate to distant places. When the middle part is high the inhabitants of the place lose a great lot of their money. When the ground (measured in a straight line) from the south-east to northwest is low people will suffer from poverty. When the ground in the middle and in the east is high, people there will prosper for the first 10 years. When the south-east and south is high, people will prosper for the first 100 years and then only losses of children will happen. When the south-east is high, prosperity will attend for 1000 years. When the west is high, prosperity will attend for 800 years. When the north-west is high, prosperity will be for only 12 years. When the north is high, prosperity will be for 8 years. When the north-east is high, prosperity will be for 6 years. All the effects mentioned before will take place only after the lapse of the above-mentioned years.

Regarding trees grown, the effects experienced are much. It is good if banyan tree and jack fruit tree are grown in the east. Tamarind is good in the south. Brahmin trees and Palmyra trees are also good in the west. Mango tree is good in the north. Naga and Palasa trees are also good in the north. If the Brahmin tree is grown in the east, the house will be burnt to ashes. When Palasa tree is grown in the south, people living in the house will become mad.

When banyan tree is grown in the west, there will be murder. When Udumbha tree is grown in the south, it is good. When it is grown in the north, people will suffer from stomach complaints. There are other effects also. Trees with strong inner fibre can be grown in the middle of the compound. Trees with strong fibre eveywhere (as teak, tamarind) can be grown only far away from the house. Weak fibred trees and trees with strong fibre in the outside can be grown only outside the compound.

Houses cannot be constructed in the back or on the left hand side of a temple where mild deities (such as Vishnu) are worshipped. Avoid houses in front of, or on the right hand side of deities who are cruel in nature (Siva, etc). Do not construct houses near paddy fields, and then there will be unexpected danger. Whenever we construct a house, we should see that the roof of the house is lower than that of temple. This much is given regarding the selection of the ground where the house has to be constructed.Regarding the construction of the building, much care has to be taken. Which quarter of the ground has to be selected?

Take a square plot and divide it into 4 padas. Eka pada is Manushya Pada (NorthEast). People living in it will prosper. Niriti Pada (Sout-West) is Deva Pada. Houses in the same are also good. Houses constructed in the South-East (Agni Khanda or Yama Khanda) are very bad. Deaths often take place here. Vayu Khanda is Asina Khanda (North-West) and this can be used for merchant's houses.

Q. 91. Explain why when the rising time of Yamakantaka is inauspicious every day, it is observed as bad only on Thursdays.

Ans. Yamakantaka is a very auspicious upagraha and anything done at that time ends only in good. But on Thursdays it is observed as inauspicious because he is believed to be an illegitimate issue of Jupiter. Still, if birth happens in his rising time it is considered as most fortunate on all days.

Q. 92. Is there any choice left when Tarabala conflicts with Chandrashtama as in the case of Anuradha and Jyeshta for Aswini?

Ans. No doubt there is a conflict in this case. If a day can be found outside the Chandrashtama period, well and good but if it is imperative that the matter has to be attempted during the Chandrashtama period, it can be expected that the result will not be as bad as otherwise because of favourable Tarabalas.

Q. 93. For beginning auspicious work which is more

important - Tarabala or Chandrabala?

Ans. Tarabala is more specific to the individual concerned and has to be given greater weight. This is fully discussed in our book ELECTIONAL ASTROLOGY.

Q. 94. Are we to take Rasi Chakra or Bhava Chakra for Muhurthas?

Ans. In South India, Rasi Chakra is being followed in Muhurtha while for horoscopy Bhava Chakra along with Rasi Chakra is being accepted. Parasara wants us to follow Bhavas and Rasi Chakra for Muhurthas also. Hence both are to be looked into.

Q. 95. What is the scientific significance of Varasoola and Rahukala?

Ans. Rahukala has been explained by the ancient astrologers thus: An evil demoness resembling 'Yogini' rises at the particular ghatikas and spreads a poisonous atmosphere all around the earth. Hence anything done at that time will end inauspiciously. Though this is the reason regarding it, modern science has not yet explained it. In South India this is observed very scrupulously when fixing all Muhurthas. We cannot brush aside Rahukala, though it has not been 'accepted' by modern science. Many things not accepted in the 19th century have been accepted in the 20th century and before the lapse of many years this will also come to the light of the day. Till then, we have to put faith in the wisdom of our ancient ancestors who have discovered and handed down to us greater things, than could be dreamt of by any modern scientists.

With regard to Varasoola there is more substantial scientific explanation. In one of the versions of PRASNA MARGA (Chapter XVI), a detailed account of 'Yogini', her shape, nature, and travels have been given. A close study of it will reveal that Varasoolas are based upon her travels. Though

'Yogini' and everything coming with her may not appeal to modern scientific thought, the effects caused by her will satisfy every one of us. You call it terrestrial magnetism or shims of the atmosphere: the effect is there and every close observer can feel it.

Stri Jataka

Q. 96. How does astrology reveal the secret of widowhood and childlessness?

Ans. Mars in the 7th house in an evil house indicates widowhood. Ketu too does the same. Venus when weak and betwixt two evil planets brings in widowhood. According to PRASNA MARGA, Saturn stands as karaka for husband in a female horoscope. If he is afflicted and joins Mars or Ketu in the 7th house, widowhood is caused.

The 8th house in a female horoscope indicates 'Mangalya'. If it is aspected by Mars or Ketu, widowhood may be expected. A benefic in the 2nd house will avert widowhood.

Childlessness is caused in many ways. It is known as Vandhya Dosha. When the Beeja. Sphuta of the husband is afflicted, his wife will be childless. When the husband is a Shanda (eunuch), the wife will be childless.

When the 9th house in a female horoscope is afflicted there will be no issue. When the 5th house in a female horoscope is afflicted, she will have no capacity to bear children. When Kshetra Sphuta is afflicted by Nava Doshas, she will not bring forth children.

Q. 97. There are many yogas dealing about the number of women which a man may keep as wives or concubines. What will be the effect if these yogas are found in a female horoscope?

Ans. Unless you find Bhanga Yogas in the female

horoscope, all the yogas mentioned can be applied.

Q. 98. Some are of the opinion that Mars is the karaka for the husband in a female horoscope. Is this correct?

Ans. According to PRASNA MARGA Saturn is the karaka. Generally Venus in a female horoscope is taken as the karaka. Mars cannot be a karaka as he governs 'blood'. Further no author, so far as I know, has accepted him as karaka for husband in a female horoscope.

Q. 99. From what houses is the character of a girl to be foretold?

Ans. There is no difference between a girl's horoscope and a boy's one regarding this. The 2nd house indicates speech. The 5th house shows the mind; the 10th house, actions. If these are afflicted, the character also is much affected. Regarding planets, the Moon and Saturn play a prominent part. Here the three gunas Satwa, Rajas and Thamas may be deducted from the position and strength of planets. Some authors include the 3rd house also as it denotes Duschilka and the 12th house as it denotes 'Durita Karma'. Again we have to note the 'Horas' (one-half of a sign) in which the planets stand. If they occupy Chandra Hora (lunar half), the nature of the person cannot be changed. If it is in Surya Hora (solar half); there can be improvement.

Readers will do well to go through PRASNA MARGA, Chapter XIV and study the nature of the Doshas seen in a person.

Q. 100. What are the combinations for loose character in a lady?

Ans. Certain yogas of Venus and Mars cause immorality. If the 7th house is badly afflicted by these planets, the woman will be immoral. If the 10th house or its lord is afflicted, the actions of the girl will be immoral. Here we have to note that the term 'immorality' is relative. It differs with defferent nations.

Q. 101. For a girl born in Libra Lagna with no planet in the 1st house and Jupiter in the 8th house, does it show widowhood?

Ans. This by itself cannot mean widowhood. On the other hand, it indicates that the husband should be long-lived or that the girl will die as a Sumangali, as Jupiter is a benefic. His being lord of the 3rd and the 6th does not matter in this connection. He is a subha planet nevertheless. The other influences in the horoscope should also be taken into consideration and no particular Bhava in isolation from the rest.

Q. 102. Is there any rule stating that the Lagna at the time of puberty will be aspected or owned by Mars and aspected or joined by the Moon?

Ans. If by puberty is meant the first menses appearing in a girl, it has to be stated that there are no satisfactory rules to determine whether the Lagna should be owned by Mars or aspected by Mars, etc. But for menses appearing in women every month, there is authority for saying that it happens when Mars aspects or is in conjunction with the Moon. There is no rule relating the Lagna at that time to the Moon or Mars.

Q. 103. How to predict in a womans horoscope that she is skilful in medicine, surgery and law?

Ans. In these things there is not much difference between a man and a woman. In addition, to what is given for men, the following rules also may be noted:

(a) If Mars is strong or the 10th house has Martian Vargas, she will be skilled in surgery.

(b) If the 9th house (house of medicine) is strong and the lord of the 9th is connected with the 10th or the lord of the 10th, she will be skilful in medicine.

(c) The Moon governs medicines.

(d) Mercury and Jupiter govern 'law'.

Q. 104. How to predict the onset of puberty in a girl's horoscope?

Ans. We have no direct authority on this question but there are general hints regarding this in BRIHAT JATAKA, Chapter IV, verse 1.

It is said that the word 'Kamini' indicates the years when the desire for sexual union begins and ends. The 15th year is the beginning and the 51st year is the end. Thus sexual instincts are supposed to last for 36 years, the period for three rounds of Jupiter. (i) When Yama Venus is aspected by Mars in the 15th year, first puberty may take place. The position of the Moon as given in that verse must also be taken into consideration. (ii) When Mars aspects the 7th house, puberty can take place. (iii) When Mars combines with or aspects the lord of the 7th, puberty can take place. All these yogas are banded down from generation to generation in the shape of 'Guru Upadesa'.But it is in their appropriate application that the astrologer's skill rests.

Q. 105. What are the combinations in one's horoscope for his wife's death as a Sumangali (before husband's death)?

Ans. There are several combinations given in ancient astrological works which may be studied with interest and advantage. However, the following important ones may be noted :

(1) Malefics in the 7th house, lord of the 7th in the 6th and lord of the 8th in the 7th cause the death of wife before the husband. (2) If the 2nd house is afflicted, then also death of the wife will be before the husband. (3) Another reliable method would be to determine the longevity of the wife assuming her Lagna to be the 7th from the husband's and see if the longevity

so obtained is less than that of the husband. (4) Death of wife as Sumangali may be anticipated if the 7th lord from the Lagna or from the owner of the Rasi occupied by the Moon is in the 12th or is in the 7th with a malefic. (5) If Saturn occupies the 7th identical with the Rasi owned by the Moon, death of wife may be predicted. (6) If the 11th and the 8th houses as measured from Venus are occupied by malefics, the wife will die early.

There are so many other considerations which have to be carefully taken into account before a prediction is ventured. You have also to distinguish between the death of the first wife (as Sumangali) and the second wife as Amangali. The line of demarcation is delicate and calls forth, on the part of the astrologer, great skill and intuition.

Q. 106. How to predict obscure and incestuous debauchery in a female horoscope?

Ans. Study the disposition of Venus and Mars or examine the Vargas of the 7th house. If Mars and Venus are ill-disposed and occupy adrisya rasis (invisible signs), predict the above effects. The lord of the 7th also must have the above-mentioned position and affliction.

Q. 107. If the wife has no horoscope of her own, can her death be predicted from the horoscope of her husband?

Ans. A good astrologer must, though it may involve very difficult calculations, predict the same correctly.

Q. 108. How far are the principles dealing with harlotry and prostitution as given in BHAVA KUTHUHALA be relied upon?

Ans. Jivanatha, the great author of BHAVA KUTHUHALA, cannot mislead us in any way. If the yogas mentioned there exist in a horoscope, they should come to pass. The error is not with the author but with the reader.

Q. 109. In some parts of India, Ritu Jataka (puberty horoscope) is important and the birth chart is ignored, while almost all astrological treatises deal only with female horoscopes and not Ritu Jataka. Why?

Ans. Ritu Jataka is only one of the charts that can be prepared in reading the life of a female. In places where Ritu Jataka alone prevails, birth is ignored not because it is unimportant but because the custom prevails there. For example, in some places, Nama Nakshatra alone prevails but not the asterism at the time of birth. In some places, horoscopes are prepared with Vivaha Muhurtha (Marriage Lagna). This does not mean that one is more important than the other. Both are effective and in fact most of the rules in female horoscopes are applied to Ritu Jataka or Vivaha Muhurtha. PRASNA MARGA wants us to look into all these for a thorough analysis.

Q. 110. If Saturn is placed in the 7th from Lagna whether aspected or not, it has Dig Bala. As per verse 8, Chapter 24 of BRIHAT JATAKA, if Saturn occupies the 7th aspected by a malefic, she lives as an unmarried maid. How do you reconcile these two results in a female horoscope?

Ans. Dig Bala is one of the important sources of strength. SARAVALI gives the following as the effects of planets having Dig Bala. (But Varaha Mihira does not give in the verse referred to above the effects of Dig Bala.) It is merely the effect of Saturn occupying the 7th, the house of marriage, aspected by malefics. If Saturn is strong in all respects and is aspected by benefics, she will marry early and lead a happy marital life.

Miscellaneous

Q. 111. Mass evacuations took place in the Punjab. Would it have been indicated in the horoscopes of those millions of people that all of them would suffer evacuation at the same time? How to predict that one is likely to be caught in such mass evacuations and sufferings like war, famine, etc.?

Ans. That a man is bound to suffer in a particular way will be indicated in his horoscope, If he is one of a family the event will be reflected in the horoscopes of others in an appropriate manner, i.e., if a son dies, the death will be indicated in the horoscope of the boy as well as in the mother's own horoscope. But in the case of a mass evacuation or mass famine, etc., there is no connection between the vast numbers of persons involved and so there is no basis to attempt any such predictions. So it is beyond the scope of natal astrology. When a country is subjected to evil rays the individual has no separate independent existence. He becomes a part of the whole and an astrologer is expected to keep a vigilant eye on the directions in the national chart as well as the effects of other celestial phenomena with the help of mundane astrology (which studies the influence of New Moons, Eclipses, Ingresses, planetary conjunctions and comets) upon the fate of nations, countries and peoples. Certain signs ascribed to the various parts of India as also to the other countries of the world will also have to be considered in this connection.

Q. 112. On what basis is the allotment of different portfolios to planets in mundane astrology made?

Ans. Samvatsaradhipa is the lord of the weekday of Samvatsara. He is the Raja or king. The minister is the lord of the weekday of Mesha Sankramana (Aries ingress). Senadhipa is the lord of the weekday of Simha Sankramana (Leo ingress). Sasyadhipa is the lord of the weekday of Kataka Sankramana (Cancer ingress). Dhanyadhipa is the lord of the weekday of

Dhanus Sankramana (Sagittarius ingress). Arghadhipa is the lord of the Weekday of Mithuna Sankramana (Gemini ingress). Meghadhipa is the lord of the weekday of Aridra Nakshatra Sankramana (Ingress into Aridra). Rajadhipa is the lord of the weekday of Thula Sankramana (Libra ingress). Neerasadhipa is the lord of the weekday of Makara Sankramana (Capricorn ingress), etc.

Q. 113. What are the favourable signs, lunar days and constellations that cause cocks and hens to produce fertile eggs?

Ans. The favourable signs are Aries, Cancer, Libra and Capricorn. The 1 st, the 7th and the 8th houses of the sign should be free. The favourable constellations are Rohini, the three Uttaras, Hasta, Swati, Anuradha, Sravana, Satabhisha, Revati and also Aswini, Mrigasira, Punarvasu, Pushya, Chitta and Dhanishta. The favourable lunar days are the 2nd, 3rd, 5th, 6th, 7th, 10th, 11th, 12th and 13th.

Q. 114. Name any astrological publication in relation to agriculture poultry-farming and animal husbandry.

Ans. Varaha Mihira has dealt with these subjects in bis own inimitable style in his immortal work BRIHAT SAMHITA.

Q. 115. What is the sign that governs Kerala?

Ans. Varaha Mihira in his BRIHAT SAMHITA has given three constellations for Kerala-Uttara, Hasta and Chitta (12th verse in the 14th chapter). Mars governs Kerala (Verse 11, Chapter XVI and Samhita).

Q. 116. How to predict civil war, famine, conquest by foreigners and attainment of independence from a country's horoscope?

Ans. In a country's horoscope, Civil War is considered from the 12th house. The 8th stands for conquest. Attainment of freedom is indicated by the Kendra and Thrikona houses with particular reference to the 10th. Then a careful study of the planetary transits and other important celestial phenomena such as conjunctions, eclipses, etc., is required. BRIHAT SAMHITA, PRASNA MARGA and HINDU PREDICTIVE ASTROLOGY are some of the works on the subject.

Q. 117. What shares are ruled by the Moon, Saturn and Ketu?

Ans. Moon-liquids (all trades depending upon liquid) and silver; Saturn-agriculture, mines and the metal lead; Ketu-all metal industries dependent upon machinery and the metal iron; Ketu has no place in Western commercial astrology, but as he is similar to Mars, what is given to Mars can be applied to Ketu also.

Q. 118. How to forecast heavy rains in a particular year?

Ans. General Rules regulating rains have been given in BRIHAT SAMHITA and PRASNA MARGA. We have to remember that rains have to be predicted differently for different places. General rules apply to all lands though the amount of rainfall may differ. In some places there will also be snowfall. Besides there are a lot of Dravidian songs (folklore) giving signs of the approaching rains. When Ravi Sankramana (solar ingress) falls in the night, rains will be scarce during that lunar month. When the Parivesha of the Moon is in the northern side, there will be no rain. When the rainbow is indistinct and seen in the North-Western side there will be no rain. Fishermen living on the coasts think that when thick mist clouds the horizon in the morning, there will be no rain that day.

Q. 119. When do the influences of planetary aspects on markets actually begin and end?

Ans. The effects begin and end according to the illumination power of the planets, viz., the Sun-7°, the Moon -4°, Mars-6°, Mercury-3½°, Jupiter-4½°, Venus-3½°, Saturn-4½° and for other planets-4°. Suppose change is expected in the market when the Sun forms a trine with Jupiter. For example, let Jupiter be in 12° Mesha (Aries), Then 12° Leo is the trine for Jupiter. The change expected by the transit of the Sun begins when the Sun enters the 5th degree of Leo (7° being the illumination limit) and ends when the Sun passes 19° Leo-the duration of the aspect being the time taken by the Sun in transiting this orb.

Q. 120. Name the planets that affect bullion when retrograde.

Ans. According to Varaha Mihira, Mars, Jupiter and Saturn affect the bullion when retrograde.

Q. 121. What shares are ruled by Mercury, Venus and Mars?

Ans. Textiles are ruled by Mercury and Venus. Shares of Motor Companies, Railways, Trams, etc., are ruled by Mars, while Venus also governs shares pertaining to silk factories and sugar companies and firms dealing with copper wire.

Q. 122. Discuss the significance of the Vernal Equinox in Mundane Astrology.

Ans. Vernal equinox means the entry of the Sun into the Sayana Aries. It is supposed to mark the astrological year. Generally Western astrologers attach great importance to this phenomenon, as the planetary positions obtaining at the time are said to indicate the trend of world events for a period of three months. In Indian astrology, vernal equinox is important for making certain astronomical observations. It has no astrological value. On the other hand, Mesha Sankramana or the entry of the Sun into constellational Aries is of great significance.

A horoscope cast for the actual moment of entry is a mirror reflecting the nature of world events likely to happen during the course of the year. Mars in the 10th house clearly signifies the outbreak of revolution and blood-shed, while Saturn in a similar situation denotes the overthrow of the Government. A true reading of the chart is a difficult matter, for in arriving at a conclusion, due care must be taken of the other planetary combinations.

Q. 123. Do planets affect market fluctuations? Are there any authoritative publications on the subject?

Ans. There is an intimate relationship between planetary movements and market fluctuations. The ancient Hindus had discovered this phenomenon long before the so-called dawn of civilisation. References about commercial astrology can be found in Varaha Mihira's BRIHAT SAMHITA, while the famous work ARGHA JATHAKA is exclusively devoted to the exposition of this branch of astrology. ARGHA JATHAKA further gives hints as to how profits can be earned by storing commodities and materials at a particular time and selling them under the influence of particular constellations. Of course, these principles have to be adapted to suit modern conditions, with care and caution. From times immemorial the Sun and the Moon are associated with gold and Silver. Whenever the Sun is subject to the evil aspects of Saturn, Rahu and Ketu the price of gold declines while the Moon under similar aspects creates a bearish tendency in, silver market. My own observations have convinced me that there is a correspondence between the gaining of latitude by the Moon and fluctuations in the silver market. Notice also that Saturn has much to do with steel.

Q. 124. How to predict rains?

Ans. This is a question very useful to modern requirements

and a scientific study of the same, with authorities to stand upon, will serve a great public purpose. There are many difficulties in handling the subject. In the first place, accepted authorities are very few. Rain cannot be considered as a general phenomenon it varies in different latitudes and places. As such Varsha Kala as understood in North India does not apply to Malabar or East Bengal. Outside India, the rainy season is quite different. As such to formulate general principles on the subject seems to be a very difficult task. Ancient Rishis had their own concept of Geography and that is embodied in the treatises on Gola. Vedas contain many verses regarding the map of the world. Since then there have been changes on the surface of the earth. Great Varaha in his BRIHAT SAMHITA is very careful regarding it and has quoted certain general principles. Desert regions have no rainfall and hence to predict rains there according to him will have no meaning. PRASNA MARGA has to say something and that too is quite meagre. Hence we are forced to take it as more a local phenomenon, and rely on the rich experience of people living in different parts of India. Thus in South India certain principles have been given by the ancients and some of them are embodied in the old folklore. Ancient peasants knew these and understood correctly when they could expect rains and when they could not. Some of these are noted below.

This part of India is a land of the South-West Monsoon and as such it has its rains in June, July and August (Taurus, Gemini and Cancer). It commences in Aries and the sowing work begins after Aries Vishu.

(1) When Mercury and Venus join in any of the Rasis, viz., Pisces, Aries, Taurus, Gemini and Cancer there will be rain.

(2) When the Sun enters the above-mentioned Rasis in the daytime there will be rain during the dark half of the month. But when he enters these in the night, there will be rain in the bright half.

(3) When the Moon joins watery Rasis, there will be rain.

(4) When the Moon joins Mars in Taurus and is aspected by Jupiter or Venus, there will be rain.

(5) When the Sun stays in the constellation Aridra, ordinarily there will be very heavy rains. This is the period of heaviest rainfall, but there should be no Bhanu Madhyama i.e. Sun should not be hemmed in between two evil planets.

(6) When Venus is aspected by Jupiter in any of the above- mentioned Rasis there will be rains.

(7) When the Moon joins more than three planets in the above-noted Rasis, there will be rains.

(8) When the ocean roars during daytime, there will be rain in the night.

(9) When the ocean is unusually calm in Pisces, there will be rains during the coming months.

(10) When the Chakora bird cries consecutively for 7 days, there will be only late rains.

(11) When Indra Dhanus (rainbow) is seen in the western sky there will be rains.

(12) When the Moon has its Parivesha, there will be rains.

(13) When crows bathe in water-pools/ puddles, there will be rains.

(14) When frogs croack during daytime, there will be rain.

Q. 125. What planets and signs govern and indicate the following:

(a) Pepper, gunny bags, jute?

(b) What is the radix for Delhi?

Ans.(a) Pepper -Sun and watery signs; gunny bags-Venus and Libra; jute-Venus and Taurus.

(b) The radix is supposed to be Scorpio.

Q. 126. .What are the indications and the lords of jute and jute products, their crop and prices?

Ans. Jute is technically under 'Karma Moola' and jute products 'Bhoga Moola'. Taurus governs jute. The Chaturthamsa (1/4th division) of Taurus governs jute products.

Venus is the planet that governs both. Prices increase when Venus occupies unfavourable positions from these. The maximum is reached when Venus is in debility and aflicted by evil planets. When malefics transit the two Rasis, crops fail. If the malefic is Mars the reason for the failure is want of rain. If the malefic is Saturn winds work havoc. The Sun disturbs the rain, floods wash away the crops.

Thus a study of Taurus and its Chaturthamsa indicate the condition of jute and crops. Venus also must be properly studied.

Q. 127. What planets rule India, Egypt, Britain, Burma, etc and how does one interpret the movements of planets in relation to national events?

Ans. India is ruled by Virgo, England by Aries and Egypt by Gemini. These rulerships seem to have been allocated by the ancients on the basis of experience. As regards rulership of the different provinces, reference may be made to the chapter on Karma Vibhaga in BRIHAT SAMHITA and to the April 1944 issue of The Astrological Magazine. National astrology is a difficult art. Predictions cannot be based merely upon the transits of planets in signs. The planetary cabinet, eclipses, positions at the time of Equinoxes, etc., have all an important bearing. Generally benefic planets transiting a particular sign would give rise to plenty and peace in the country under the dominion of the sign concerned while malefics cause results appropriate to their nature-: Mars-fires, wars, revolutions and destruction; Saturn-labour troubles, strikes, mass uprisings and so on.

Q. 128. Do the planets have any influence over beasts? If so, are the Dasas which total to 120 years applied to them? Will it be the same for beasts whose life-span is in variance with that of man?

Ans. That planets have influence over not only beasts, but over vegetable life and even mineral life is undoubted. The BRIHAT SAMHITA of Varaha Mihira is a vast storehouse of information on these topics, and astrology even in the West has been defined as "the science that investigates the action and reaction constantly going on between the celestial bodies and the rest of manifested nature, including man and reveals the laws under which this takes place.

The Dasas whether Vimshottari, Kalachakra, Nisarga or Jaimini's all have to be applied as they are to the lives of beasts also. The period has neither to be reduced nor increased even though the life-span of a particular animal is normally less or more than the average human life. This is because, the period of 120 years is based on Symbology and not because it is the normal life of a human being. The Dasas, as they are, are being applied not only to human beings but also to the time of foundation stones being laid for buildings, the first or beginning moment of societies which are generally expected to last beyond even 120 years, etc. Even if a human being lives beyond 120 years, it has to be applied in the same way.

Q. 129. Do stones really have any effect?

Ans. Precious stones when properly selected and used to ward off evils indicated by the planets. Different planets have different stones. A proper use of them will also help the native in favourable situations or enterprises. Varaha Mihira devotes a chapter on the natural effects of precious stones.

Q. 130. What remedial measures will you suggest for

the following diseases: (a) Tuberculosis; (b) Madness; (c) Leprosy?

Ans. These are terrible diseases and the medical aspect is outside our scope. Generally medicines fail to cure these not because Ayurveda is defective but the root cause is ignored. Past Karmas have brought these and they are to be looked into and remedial measures adopted. Sayanacharya has detailed on these and PRASNA MARGA gives a short summary. Here I shall give the measures recommended by the great author of VEERASIMHAVALOKANA, a medical treatise as well.

Tuberculosis: Persons who bring about murder of good people in previous birth get this disease. One who misappropriates temple-wealth gets this. As a remedial measure, make a plantain (Kadali Rambha) tree in gold and present the same to a good and virtuous man with mantras. You can make an image of a man with this disease in gold and give it free to a good man with chanting of mantras. Attend to Chandrayana Vratas (rites) carefully for six years. Then you will be free.

Madness: This is caused in two ways. As a result of Ahhichara (black-magic) this has to be cured by removing the Abhichara by suitable mantraic rites. This is accidental and is caused by enemies. Secondly, sins such as stealing, plagiarism and incendiarism also bring about this disease, As a remedial measure, the patient should be taken to temples of repute and dragged around the temple buildings.

Leprosy: One who steals, gold gets this disease. As a remedial measure, give free Umamaheswara Pratima (image) made in gold or silver with mantras. Feed poor people free. After attending to these, begin medical treatment and the medicines will be effective.

Q. 131. What are the sastraic remedies for averting the evil effect of a malefic Venus Dasa?

Ans. Doshas (evil effects) of planets are generally removed by prayers, worship, Homas, etc. Before we attempt to remove the evil effects, we should analyse the planet and find out its nature. Venus in his Satvic forms represents Annapoorneswari or Lakshmi. In its Thamasic form, he rules Durga or Kali or any lower deity indulging in harming mankind. Having ascertained its nature, we should resort to propitiate it by worship or prayers. The science of remedies is complicated and dangerous and you should leave it to experts.

Q. 132. Astrology is said to be a science of indications and not one of destiny. How to find out astrologically that one will not heed astrological forebodings? For example, say it is predicted for one that he will marry a rich girl before a certain date and he neglects good opportunities before that date. Can such a mentality on the part of one be predicted?

Ans. It is true that the science of astrology is a science of indications. Provided there is a strong will and requisite effort is brought into play, certain indications in the horoscope can be overcome. Of course, the strong will in such a case will be indicated in the nativity itself, just as unfavourable indications can be overcome. In the above manner, the promise of good effects can also be spoiled in various ways. A weak and vacillating mind will not be able to take advantage of the planetary vibrations and bring them to fruit. In the example cited, if the man acts perversely, he can prevent a good alliance by marriage. It is to some extent within the range of prediction. Such a result will happen if Lagnadhipa (Ascendant lord) is weak by sign, house position, or combust.

Q. 133. The use of precious stones in accordance with the strength of the Lagna lord is advocated by you, while others advocate the selection of a gem appropriate to the evil planet in question. Please elucidate.

Ans. My recommendation is based on the consideration that a gem appropriate to the Lagna lord would act as a protective shield. It is like maintaining one's general health good.Wearing a precious stone consistent with the nature of malefic planet wards off the evils due to it during its Dasa and Bhukti. This may be compared to treatment given to a particular disease one is suffering from.

Q. 134. State how Balarishta is averted?

Ans. Balarishta Yogas are of three kinds : (1) Yogaja, (2) Niyatha, (3) Aniyatha.1 and 3 can be averted by suitable remedies. Find out the planets which cause Balarishta from the horoscope. See where they stand, whether in Chandra or Surya Hora. If they occupy the former, the arishta cannot be averted. If the latter, Prayaschittams (remedies) may remove the evil in most cases.

Q. 135. How to predict our previous Karma?

Ans. The cumulative effect of our previous karma is our present birth. The birth chart indicates the previous sins and merits through planets. When the planets are weak and occupy bad positions, we can conclude that we have committed more sins than merits. If some planets are favourable, we can say we have done more meritorious work. In Prasnas, the 9th house is analysed taking it as Lagna. The 9th house-Karma Swarupa, the 10th Karma Dhana, the 11th Karma Sahaya, the 12th Karma Adhikarana, the 1st Karma Bhutha Vasthu, the 2nd Karma Nasa Karana, the 3rd Karma Sahachari, the 4th Karmayus, the 5th Karma Bhagya, the 6th Karma Vyapara, the 7th Karma Labha, and the 8th is Karma Vyaya.

Q. 136. What is the best astrological treatise on remedial measures?

Ans. The treatise of Sayanacharya is the best available one. PRASNA MARGA and VEERASIMHAVALOKANA are equally good.

Q. 137. Why is fasting prescribed only on certain days such as Sankranti, Amavasya, etc.?

Ans. Fasting has been prescribed for Grahasthas or householders on two types of days, Pitru Dina and Daiva Dina. For Sanyasis or ascetics no day-injunction has been made. In the chapter on "Kshetra Prasna", the author of PRASNA MARGA prescribes fasting as a remedial measure for sins done in the past birth. The days prescribed are considered holy in the sense that your 'Karmas' done then meet with least resistance when transmitted through this opaque world. On other days, the performer's ego is covered with Thamas (inertia) and the world too is in Thamas.

Q. 138. Do you agree with all the rules in Maharnava?

Ans. The question is not clear. If you mean some of the remedial measures suggested by the great author are not efficacious, I disagree with the question. Most of the 'Prayaschittas' mentioned are Vedic in nature and will bear fruit if they are performed by real Brahmins. There is nothing wrong with the rules but unfortunately we have not got sound priests to perform them. Rishi Prokta cannot be questioned since they (Rishis) wrote unselfishly with no base motives.

Q. 139. Astrologers suggest opals, moonstone and sapphires as lucky stones to wear. When there are nine stones (Navratnas) why should the above stones be specified and which planets rule these stones?

Ans. It is true that Navratnas are recommended in our ancient treatises. Opals, moon-stone, and sapphire are of recent transports from the rear east. The Chaldeans had these stones in their ancient texts. As such, we cannot brush aside them as of no astrological value.

Coral is ruled by Mars; Topaz is ruled by Jupiter; Sapphire is governed by Saturn; Ruby is governed by the Sun; Emerald is governed by Mercury; Pearl is governed by the Moon; and

Diamond is governed by Venus.

Q. 140. Can the evil effects of a Dasa be averted by sastraic remedies even if that planet is in manhood stage (tharuna).If so, to what extent?

Ans. The evil effect of planets can be averted or modified by suitable astrological remedies. Prayaschitta is a science by itself and great venerable Rishis have devoted considerable time and space to think out these and their works remain even today in spite of all destruction and opposition. Even if the planet is in Tharuna, the evil effects can be modified but it requires more effective measures. Dasas reveal to us the effect of our past actions done deliberately (Dridha Karma) and the malefic effects can be considerably modified.

Q. 141. Why should Jupiter prove harmful when he transits the Jamna Rasi while doing good when placed in Lagna or in Moon sign?

Ans. The sign refers to transits or Gochara Phala and affects only that particular year, whereas the 2nd pertains to Jataka or actual chara and house of different significance.

Q. 142. For all births from Aries to Pisces, Jupiter the natural benefic has some or other defects with reference to lordship. Discuss the effects.

Ans. Jupiter, the natural benefic, becomes wholly evil when he owns Kendras (quadrants) for Gemini, Virgo, Sagittarius or Pisces. He is also wholly evil when the Lagna is Taurus, Libra or Capricorn as he then becomes the owner of the 8th and the 11th, the 3rd and the 6th and the 3rd and the 12th Bhavas respectively. For other Lagnas namely Aries, Cancer, Leo, Scorpio and Aquarius, he is mixed in nature. Jupiter is best by ownership for Aries Lagna as he then becomes lord of the 9th and the 12th.

Q. 143. Define Elarata Influence.

Ans. This influence begins when Saturn enters by transit the 12th sign from the Moon after birth, and lasts till he leaves the second sign from that Rasi. As he normally remains in each sign for 2½ years, this period extends to 3 x 2½ = 7½ years. The whole period is not favourable and all sorts of evils may be experienced subject to current natal directions. But if Saturn is favourable and strong in the nativity, the troubles experienced will be correspondingly less. This elarata can occur thrice in a man's career at intervals of 30 years. The first cycle is considered very bad, second not so bad, even good , and the third cycle is generally supposed to cause death. Not all the 7½ years will be bad.

Q. 144. Should the Vedha houses be considered while giving 'predictions' according to Gochara (transits)?

Ans. Both 'Vedha' and 'Vipareetha Vedha' should be looked into. According to PRASNA MARGA (9-22-49), "Whoever reads 'Bhava Phala' without looking into 'Vedha and Vipareetha Vedha' will have his predictions proving untrue".

Q. 145. Rasi effects in the case of Gochara are general. Will not Bhava play a more prominent part in the case of Gochara effects?

Ans. The Rishis who expounded the Gochara effects have significantly not applied transits to the Bhavas but only to the signs as counted from the place of the birth Moon. The transits of planets in Bhavas from Lagna will not be without effects and are tried in Western Astrology, i.e., evil planets transiting a particular Bhava affect the matters indicated by that Bhava adversely and benefics favourably: But in practice, they are not found to operate with that uncanny accuracy as in the case of Gochara results as traditionally interpreted.

Q. 146. Define Lattas and their importance in

Gochara.

Ans. Lattas are of two kinds, viz., Pure Lattas or forward afflictions caused by the Sun, Mars, Jupiter and Saturn and Prishta Lattas or backward afflictions caused by the Moon, Mercury, Venus and Rahu. The 12th, 3rd, 6th and the 8th stars counted from the Sun, Mars, Jupiter and Saturn respectively are Lattas for the respective planets. Similarly the 5th, 7th, 9th and the 2nd stars counted from Venus, Mercury, Rahu and the Moon respectively become Lattas for the respective planets.

Let us assume that the Sun is transiting Aswini (Aries) happening to be the 11th from one's Janma Rasi (Gemini). Suppose at the same time Mars is transiting Uttara-the 12th star from Aswini, evidently the Sun is subject to Latta. This neutralises all the good influences due to the Sun's presence in the 11th and causes quite the contrary effects. Both good and evil planets when subject to Latta give rise to adverse results. When there is more than one Latta, at the same time the combined effects will increase in intensity. The pure Lattas should be counted in the clockwise direction and the Prishta Latta in the anti-clockwise or reverse direction. Thus, if Venus is in Mrigasira, any planet simultaneously transiting Aswini (5th counted backwards) would cause Latta to Venus. A consideration of the Latta factor is very important for correctly appreciating the results due to transits.

Q. 147. If the lord of one, Saturn is exalted and posited in a Trikona (trine), will he cast his beneficial influence in transits?

Ans. Such a Saturn will shed beneficial influences when he passes through the 3rd, 6th, 10th and 11th houses. When he passes through other houses, he will be neutral.

Q. 148. The transit of Saturn over the radical Saturn will adversely affect the native. Transit over the 8th house

is also bad. Will the results be the same if Saturn is lord of the 1st and occupies the 8th house?

Ans. The said transit of Saturn as a planet is bad. Mantreswara is of opinion that the lord of the 1st whoever he may be is benefic in nature. As such the transit of Saturn as lord of the 1st over the 8th house will not be fully unfavourable.

Q. 149. Period of sadesati is considered to be bad-of the three rounds, the 2nd round. Do you agree with this?

Ans. Period of Sadesati is usually bad. There are three rounds in one's life. Of these, the first and the third are bad. The 2nd may sometimes be favourable. This view is generally considered to be sound. The 2nd round begins in one's 30 or 31st year and the 32nd year of one's life is considered to be one of the turning points. Chandra Lagna (Moon-sign) begins to make it felt after the first round and Surya Lagna (Sun-sign) after the 2nd, i.e., 60th year. It is during these periods Hindus are enjoined to perform Prayaschittas remedial measures as Dwatrimsa Mrityunjaya Homa or Shashti Poorthi Rudra Puja, etc. The second round of Saturn Sadesati is considered to be good in the sense that the 7½ years then will not be as unfavourable to the native as the other two periods.If Saturn is bad in the horoscope all the three periods will be bad. If Saturn is favourable at the time of birth, the 2nd period will be more favourable than 1 and 3, i.e., 1st and 3rd periods will be neutral. Why it is so has not been explained by Parasara. There is however a saying that the 2nd round will generally see the native turning more Godly. Sense effects are replaced by Atmaic effects.

Whatever be the reason, this view has to be accepted because it has been accepted as Pramana (axiomatic) though written records are not found.

Q.150. If Jupiter posited in transit in the 8th from

the Moon and in the 10th from Lagna, what will be the Gochara effects?

Ans. In Gochara, we generally look into whether it is posited in favourable places from Janma Rasi (Moon-sign). But if we wish to have an accurate study of the nature of the effects in Gochara, we ought to see whether that particular planet is in a favourable house from Janma Lagna, from the Rasi occupied by the Sun at the time of birth and from the Rasis occupied by the other planets a time of birth. This is exactly what we do in working out Ashtakavarga Tables. For example, if we find 5 points in the 8th house from the Moon in the Ashtakavarga Tables of Jupiter, we conclude that that place is 5/8 good and 3/8 bad and Gochara effect of Jupiter will be 5/8 good and it is even possible by analysing the table to say when the good effects will happen.

Q. 151. What is Kantaka Sani (Saturn) in Gochara?

Ans. Transit of Saturn in the 4th, 7th and the 10th Rasis from the Moon-sign is said to be Kantaka.

Q. 152. How are transfers of Government servants to be predicted from Gochara position of planets?

Ans. Planets in Dusthanas (the 6th, the 8th and the 12th) without Vedha or Vipareetha Vedha bring about transfers causing discomfort, expenditure and anxiety. Planets in good positions bring in transfers giving additional comfort, income and general happiness. Planets in Dusthanas with Vedha or planets in Susthanas with either Vedha or Vipareetha Vedha cause simple transfers. The individual is not affected in either way.

Q. 153. What are the special circumstances under which Elarata may do good to the native?

Ans. If Saturn has Vedha or if Saturn is unusually strong at the time of birth he will do good to the native.

Q. 154. Will the Sadesati give malefic results all along his period? If Saturn is a Yoga karaka, what will be the nature of the period? Will there be any signs in the body of the native who undergoes Sadesati?

Ans. No, the first five years, i.e., while Saturn is in the 12th and the 1st, the period will be bad. But if Saturn is a Yogakaraka or when there are more than five Bindus in the Rasis indicated by the 12th and the 1st from Chandra Lagna (the Moon-sign), the effects will be least felt. Still the influence is there. This is a Gochara influence and as such Adridhakarma phalas of the native will be experienced during the Gochara period. If Saturn is weak in all respects, he will make the native either maimed or sick below the thighs or below the knees.